Praise for *Corporate Concinnity in the Boardroom*

"We need a new word in the boardroom and we have found it in 'concinnity.' Nancy Falls gives us a fresh framework for governing that will help us steward enterprises to their best performance outcomes—while maintaining that delicate balance of courage and humility required to serve well."

—Cheryl Bachelder, CEO of Popeyes Louisiana Kitchen, Inc. and author
of *Dare to Serve: How to Drive Superior Results by Serving Others*

"*Corporate Concinnity in the Boardroom* is the best book I have read about effective boards of directors. Learn best practices in selecting members, setting direction, keeping focus, and resolving conflict. If I had read this book thirty years ago I would have been more effective as chairman of my company."

—Joe Scarlett, retired chairman, Tractor Supply Company

"*Corporate Concinnity in the Boardroom,* a breakthrough governance book, creates a wonderful new framework for governing by focusing exclusively on ways to make sure that the CEO and the board are on the same page. There is expected tension between leadership and governance, but Nancy Falls has created a new framework that hits these tensions head-on, by exploring such topics as respective expectations and communication styles."

—Lynn Shapiro Snyder, Esq., Member and Director,
Epstein Becker & Green; President of Women Business
Leaders of the U.S. Health Care Industry foundation™

"Forward-thinking governance leverages relationships to identify leading indicators and key disruptive market trends, as well as to integrate strategy into governance. Nancy Falls's *Corporate Concinnity in the Boardroom* is the timely and relevant roadmap to leveraging those relationships into accelerated execution, exceptional performance, and quantifiable results."

—David Nour, senior leadership and board advisor, best-selling author
of *Relationship Economics and Return on Impact*

"*Corporate Concinnity in the Boardroom* by Nancy Falls is an important book about how to maximize the performance of companies. Falls provides common sense guidance for members of boards of directors that is worth its weight in gold. Anyone who serves on a board would be well served to read this fine book."

—Hap Klopp, founder and former CEO of The North Face,
author, lecturer, and serial entrepreneur

"With a single word, 'concinnity,' Nancy Falls's landmark book captures the complex set of dynamics and qualities that enable true professional discourse. The book illuminates a concept, a goal, and most importantly, provides a clear framework for achieving this cherished balance of unique individual contributions and like-minded leadership. I've been privileged to observe Concinnity in the Boardroom, and believe the deep insights the author conveys through examples and imperatives should serve as a rallying cry for all leaders to strive for and demand nothing less than concinnity within their teams."

—Suzanne Vautrinot, Major General (retired),
United States Air Force and board member of Symantec,
Ecolab Inc., and Parsons Corporation

"In ten concise chapters, outlining ten mandates for boards and management teams, Nancy Falls provides incredibly frank and insightful views into the dynamics of the boardroom and the C-suite. In a crowded governance marketplace, this is a must read for CEOs, chairs, and board members."

—James Bradford, former dean of the Vanderbilt University Owen
Graduate School of Business and board member of
Cracker Barrel, Clarcor, Genesco, and Granite Inc.

"*Corporate Concinnity in the Boardroom* is a breakthrough in governance and leadership practice. Nancy Falls brings a sixteenth-century concept into the boardroom and the C-suite to show us with striking simplicity how to drive results, improve lives, and have more fun in the process."

—Marshall Goldsmith, a Thinkers50 "Top Ten Global Business Thinker,"
best-selling author, and top-ranked executive coach

CORPORATE
CONCINNITY
IN THE BOARDROOM

---

10 IMPERATIVES TO DRIVE
HIGH-PERFORMING COMPANIES

NANCY FALLS

GREENLEAF
BOOK GROUP PRESS

Published by Greenleaf Book Group Press
Austin, Texas
www.gbgpress.com

Distributed by Greenleaf Book Group

For ordering information or special discounts for bulk purchases, please contact Greenleaf Book Group at PO Box 91869, Austin, TX 78709, 512.891.6100.

Design and composition by Greenleaf Book Group and Debbie Berne
Cover design by Greenleaf Book Group and Debbie Berne
Cover image: ©iStock/mattjeacock

Publisher's Cataloging Publication Data is available.

ISBN: 978-1-62634-201-9

Part of the Tree Neutral® program, which offsets the number of trees consumed in the production and printing of this book by taking proactive steps, such as planting trees in direct proportion to the number of trees used: www.treeneutral.com

TreeNeutral®

Printed in the United States of America on acid-free paper

15 16 17 18 19 20   10 9 8 7 6 5 4 3 2 1

First Edition

Other Edition(s):
eBook ISBN: 978-1-62634-202-6

con·cin·ni·ty *noun* \kən-ˈsi-nə-tē\ The skillful and harmonious arrangement or fitting together of the different parts of something (first known use: 1531)

—OXFORD ENGLISH DICTIONARY

Finding good players is easy.
Getting them to play as a team is another story.

—*Casey Stengel*

CONTENTS

The Leadership and Governance Imperative

> CORPORATE GOVERNANCE: The framework through which a board of directors helps a company meet its goals and objectives while simultaneously ensuring that it meets its obligations to multiple stakeholders. It is also the system of rules, practices, and processes by which a company is directed.

I COULD TELL the guy was sweating bullets. Despite trying to sound in control and unhurried, he was clearly in a panic to solve a management crisis brewing in the company whose board he chaired. What was not obvious from our first phone call was that his corporate house was on fire, eaten up with the flames of both leadership and governance problems.

A trusted advisor to the board had reached out to me when he found out this company was thinking about making a CEO change. Knowing they had concerns about others in the C-suite as well, the advisor thought we'd be perfect. I agreed. *Right up my alley*, I thought. So I rang him up. In speaking to the director, it became clear that their concerns were not just about the CEO and other members of the leadership team, but also about performance, which had begun to show signs of weakness.

Worse, the company had regulators nipping at its heels for alleged violations. I listened intently to all of the gory details. Thinking, *Okay, I got this,* I replied, "The bad news is that these sorts of problems are all too common in the C-suite; the good news is our company helps clients manage such situations all day long." I was confident that we could help and told him he was not to worry.

The company hired us and my team began to design and execute on a project to rectify the company's operational and regulatory issues. We soon realized, however, that "incompetent" was the nicest term we could apply to the leaders in question. We were pretty sure they knew that the regulatory matters were mission-critical, and yet the company was not even set up to handle them properly. We were less sure that they understood they were facing "someone goes to jail"-level problems.

The project got bigger, but we made progress. When it came time to present our findings and our plan to the board of directors, we were ready. We had made great strides on leadership, operations, and regulatory fronts. But it was going to take a large-scale, coordinated effort to straighten things out. We proposed an extremely compelling plan of action to the board, so we expected full concurrence, if not a few kudos for the progress we'd made.

About halfway through that first board meeting, I got a huge sinking feeling in my stomach. We had already dealt with more than we'd bargained for in terms of challenges for the company. But it was now becoming abundantly clear that all of our concerns about management paled in comparison to the issues we saw in how the board itself governed the company. The list of governance missteps was long, but perhaps the most damaging issue was the lack of mutual trust among board members.

The discomfort around the table was palpable—maybe not at the "hate your guts"–level, but close.

> Leadership is the process of utilizing appropriate "hard" skills (e.g., legal, financial, marketing, operations) and "soft" skills (e.g., decision making, communication, self management, political acumen) to influence people in driving toward stated company goals.

I'm no Pollyanna—I don't think you have to like your colleagues so much that you want to play eighteen holes of golf with them or go out for a beer on a regular basis. But mutual respect and trust are table stakes for a functioning work relationship. Sadly, they were not evident on this board. This would thus preclude our getting traction on solutions to resolve the crisis. It had already led to disagreements on the board about previously considered actions to turn things around.

Creating consensus without mutual trust and respect is impossible in times of trouble. Companies arrive at the breaking point because in good times, the absence of mutual trust and respect disappears in the noise of positive earnings, growth, and self-congratulations. The reality is that without mutual trust and respect, no board can build a governance platform capable of driving growth and success, even in good times.

Without good leadership or good governance, this company was doomed. It was a real shame; the company had done many things well. Some of the executives were quite good, and some pretty smart people sat on the board. They just did not have a handle on the two most important success factors: leadership and governance.

Why Do Leadership and Governance Matter . . . to You?

This is just one story among dozens; I've lived with and through many a good or bad leadership or governance situation. Good leadership and good governance are mission-critical—period. I am here to tell you that nothing can kill a company faster than bad leadership and poor governance.

Now, at the risk of stating the obvious, let me say that no company is perfect. None of those I have worked for or have come to know well as a trusted advisor have been flawless. In fact, I am not interested in perfect; I am interested in high performance. Over decades of experience, I have learned that good leadership and good governance **are THE defining traits of high-performing companies.** Most of the companies I've worked with or in had at least one of these things right. The few that got both wrong inevitably failed to thrive.

> Good leadership and good governance **are THE defining traits of high-performing companies.**

Yes, companies must get a lot of things right, but master good leadership and good governance and the odds of surviving—in fact, excelling—improve measurably. Get them wrong and it's almost impossible to succeed. *Nothing should be more important to you than building exceptional, sustainable leadership teams; effective, continuously improving governance platforms; and a strategy to make them work well together.*

This book offers a new approach to making leadership teams and boards of directors work well together. I call it *Corporate Concinnity.* It is a new way of governing and leading together that emphasizes harmony, ensures better CEO-board relations, and produces better corporate performance. It is easy for C-suites and boards to do battle. The Corporate Concinnity framework takes the would-be power struggles and turns them into reasons to come together through strategic alignment of the dynamic personalities and diverse skill sets within boards of directors and C-suites. The Corporate Concinnity framework's emphasis on harmony is not to be confused with complacency, apathy, or rubber-stamping of management's agenda. It is just as easy for C-suites and boards to leave each other completely alone, making decisions without discussion, mutual understanding, and consensus. True Concinnity requires a level commitment to honesty and full engagement that not only powers performance, but creates the stuff of personal legacies of significant contribution.

> Nothing should be more important to you than building exceptional, sustainable leadership teams; effective, continuously improving governance platforms; and a strategy to make them work well together.

Companies and their boards are operating in increasingly complex and risky environments. The *what* of board work has and must continue to change as a result, with increased involvement in strategy and risk management. The *who* of board work is beginning to and must change as well, including more deliberate skill-matching, board rotation, succession planning, and diversity. Most of all, the *way* boards and company management work together has never been more important, not just to navigate the risks of complexity and change, but also to create and take advantage of the opportunities inherent in those risks.

Corporate governance will be the functional imperative

of tomorrow's high-performing company. Boards that govern according to yesterday's norms—both the *what* and the *who*, but more importantly the *how*—will find it more difficult to thrive. Those that approach governance from a command and control perspective, those that see power struggles instead of calls for consensus, will not be the drivers of high-performing companies.

> Corporate governance will be the functional imperative of tomorrow's high-performing company.

Reframing Leadership

Leadership, perhaps the better understood of the two critical success factors, is about people. It is often defined as the ability of a company's management to make sound decisions and inspire others to perform well.[1] I define leadership as the process of utilizing appropriate "hard" and "soft" skills to influence people in driving toward stated company goals. Hard skills are such things as legal, financial, marketing, and operations skills; soft skills include decision making, communication, self-management, political acumen, and the like. Good leadership consists of groups of people who possess both these skill sets and deploy them effectively as a team, with mutual trust and respect. Sustainable, good leadership is about building enough robustness into the team at the top that it can survive the accelerating pace of all types of change, including changes on the team itself.

....

1   Investopedia.com.

Redefining Governance

I've had really smart investors and board types give me blank stares when I bring up the subject of governance. The denial—or worse, annoyance—those stares convey in a second's time never ceases to amaze me. Part of the problem is the lack of a widely understood *and* appreciated definition of corporate governance. Many of the most common definitions focus (often solely) on the "C word": Control. Control gained considerable traction as the definition of governance with the regulatory response to corporate scandals such as Enron and HealthSouth, and after the failures of financial giants Bear Stearns, Countrywide, AIG, and Merrill Lynch.[2] Sarbanes-Oxley and Dodd-Frank, legislation intended to solve corporate America's problems, are all about controlling the perceived bad actors among corporations.

Certainly, control as part of governance is not entirely inappropriate, but the obsessive focus on that element has meant that the very word can produce fear, even loathing, in the minds and hearts of corporate leadership. As a result many CEOs and leadership teams resist diving into the governance

....

2   I believe that defining corporate governance as solely about control falls far from the mark. After the Great Recession, as many looked for someone to blame and others scrambled for solutions, additional regulation became a popular solution. Some years later, it is easy to forget that the largest economy in the world teetered on the verge of collapse, and dramatic measures were necessary to prevent such a collapse. If there had been more control over the bad actors, all of this would not have happened (at least according to conventional wisdom in the public and in Washington, DC). Enter Sarbanes-Oxley, one of the most comprehensive pieces of financial reform legislation since the Great Depression. Undoubtedly there were unchecked excesses prior to the financial crisis. And of course not all regulation is bad. But Sarbanes-Oxley cut a very wide swath of new controls as it aimed to rein in excesses. One consequence, intended or not, is that the sole focus of corporate governance became just that: focused only on control.

dialogue. This is unfortunate, because their avoidance makes the board's job that much harder. Additionally, boards, especially the non-public variety, tend to view control in governance as an impediment to practicality in running a company. In my experience, venture capital and private equity firms often feel their size and timeframes negate the need for "all that corporate governance stuff." (It has also been my observation that many of those folks remain on the left side of the performance bell curve.) Unfortunately, such resistance makes it that much harder for their management teams to work with them.

I believe corporate governance is best defined as the framework through which a board of directors helps a company meet its goals and objectives while simultaneously ensuring that it meets its obligations to multiple stakeholders. Good corporate governance involves the harmonious arrangement of people, processes, and systems to balance the diverse goals of stakeholders as the company goes about the work of achieving its goals.

Governance generally refers to what boards of directors do. The board governs, while management leads. There is a fine but important line between governance and leadership. *In order to sustain good leadership and good governance, the line between them must be adequately communicated, thoroughly understood, and well respected.*

If you think there is not much or enough written about governance, you are not alone. There are a few good books on the basics of governance, such as *Answering the Call* and *Claiming Your Place at the Boardroom Table*.[3] However, many

3   Lynn Shapiro Snyder and Robert D. Reif, *Answering the Call: Understanding the Duties, Risks, and Rewards of Corporate Governance*, 4th ed. (Washington, DC: Women Business Leaders, 2011); Thomas Bakewell, *Claiming Your Place at the Boardroom Table* (New York: McGraw Hill, 2014).

available books are virtual textbooks on the topic, both scholarly and legal in tone. They offer valuable insight, but most operators—and I consider myself one—get pretty impatient with lengthy treatises. We are looking for concepts we can grab hold of quickly and put to use operationally for the betterment of our companies and our people—and fast.

That is exactly what this book provides. I identify common governance problems and outline straightforward operational solutions for solving them. The only aspect of my proposed Corporate Concinnity framework that is difficult to implement is the requirement that you let go of conventional definitions of governance (command and control) that focus on differences and foster conflict. But for forward-thinking boards, C-suite members, family-business owners, investors, and up-and-comers who want to be prepared when their time arrives to lead and govern, this book provides a governance how-to that ensures high performance. *It is written for the board member who wants to work well with his or her CEO.* In fact, I almost titled this book, *How to Lose a CEO in Ten Days*, because the framework I outline was born of observations of behaviors that came close to doing just that.

> This book identifies common governance problems and outlines straightforward operational solutions for solving them.

I wrote this book so that leadership and governance crises won't derail you, your company, your leadership team, or your board. My approach uses a little "tongue-in-cheekiness" to address the ten most egregious errors I've observed boards make with their CEOs, as well as what I've seen the best-performing companies do. The stories come from real, honest-to-goodness cases I've worked on with actual companies (or, in some cases, composites of companies). I have changed certain names and facts to protect the innocent, as well as the guilty. I hope you come away understanding what good corporate governance is, what it's not, and how to engage in it with a commitment to continuous improvement.

Someone to Help You See What You Can't See on Your Own

I could also have titled this book, *What You Learned When You Let Me Help You See What You Could Not See on Your Own*. I have made a career out of helping companies get leadership and governance right. I was able to see what they were not able to see themselves. As a process-oriented person with a passion for corporate performance, I've helped many a company connect the dots between cause and effect in producing results. Having been an officer of two different public companies and a member of the C-suite in others, I've seen firsthand which elements are critical to good performance. Working in financial services and in human capital, I have advised the boards, owners, and leaders of scores of companies. I have been in and around a number of organizations that did many things well. I have worked with many that got a lot of things wrong. I have learned most of what I know about leadership and governance while leading and governing with extraordinary colleagues, clients, and fellow board members. And I have good news for you: The most common corporate governance mistakes are just that—common. By approaching governance in a different way, you can avoid most of them.

What This Book Can Help You See

Let me return to the board horror story that opened this chapter. The truth is, it didn't have to be that way. These were not inexperienced, unintelligent executives, nor was it their first rodeo. They just didn't see governance as a mission-critical part of what they had to work out. They were living proof that ignorance and mismanagement in corporate governance *can* hurt you, your company, your employees, your shareholders, and other stakeholders. What this company didn't know, didn't think about, and did wrong in the governance arena devastated them.

While the most common governance mistakes can be avoided, that won't happen by just wishing it so or by assuming you have it covered by what has become conventional wisdom. C-suites and boards often go to war; just read the headlines about battles and lawsuits taking place in, among, and between those people responsible for leading and guiding corporate America's resources. Given how often it occurs, you would think such conflict is par for the course, but it is not; it is the wrong way to govern. This is true for all companies, not just small, new, private, or family-owned companies. In fact, a former board member of a *Fortune* 500 Company encouraged me to write this book because he felt *that* company didn't get corporate governance right. In other words, he has witnessed corporate governance awareness problems at the highest levels in business.

Fighting your way to agreement in governance is neither pretty nor fun. Once you set up a framework that actually pulls together the people, processes, and systems in an agreeable way, agreement follows. The best governance embraces differences as reasons to learn and grow, not to fight. My framework for *Corporate Concinnity in the Boardroom* is the best defense against the most common mistakes. The following diagram summarizes them.

Ten Common Governance Mistakes

1. Failure to clarify roles and responsibilities between the CEO/C-suite and the board.

2. Failure to get the right people around the boardroom table, fully engaged, and doing the right things.

3. Failure to develop consensus in detail about where you are, where you are going, and how you will get there.

4. Failure to tend carefully to the interests of multiple, diverse stakeholders.

5. Failure to be deliberate about exactly what information the board needs to do its job.

6. Failure to be clear on the board's responsibility for culture and its role with the CEO in managing and changing it.

7. Failure to get CEO and C-suite compensation right.

8. Failure to understand CEO (and C-suite) need for a coach and the board's very different role as the boss.

9. Failure to appreciate the inevitability of CEO, C-suite, and boardroom turnover, and inadequate efforts to keep it positive.

10. Failure to actively cultivate wisdom in the boardroom: thinking vs. doing, reflecting vs. reacting, compassion vs. insensitivity and uncaring.

Each of the ten most common governance mistakes has its origins in failure to be deliberate in pursuing consensus, to work together in harmony, and to approach corporate governance through concinnity. Step one is certainly awareness. An important second step is accepting that good governance is a journey, whether you have deep experience or are new to it. Those who do it well seek sustained excellence and appreciate that it is ongoing. It is by no means a been-there-done-that, got-it-figured-out sort of thing. And it is a journey you take with others who may or may not share your depth of experience or views.

Even if you have successfully built a governance platform for your company, even if you understand the imperative of sustainability in good governance, and even if you already believe in continuous improvement, this book is still for you.

Practicing governance through Corporate Concinnity not only makes you a far more effective director, but also builds harmony with all other stakeholders and makes the process easier and more fun. *If you never thought you could find actual joy in governing a corporation, I think you will find that the Corporate Concinnity framework for overcoming the ten most common governance mistakes will actually make that possible.*

And, after all . . . who doesn't need a little more joy in life? Enjoy!

A New Framework for Governing

#1 Draw a Line in the Sand

#2 Don't Go Overboard

#3 Assemble at the Same Starting Blocks

#4 Mind the Stakeholder Gap

#5 Manage Your Information Appetite

#6 Be Prepared: Culture and Change Readiness

#7 Don't Leave Compensation to the Experts

#8 Bench Your Inner Coach

#9 Off-Board Well

#10 Cultivate Wisdom

Draw a Line in the Sand

You don't have to worry about burning bridges if you're building your own. —KERRY E. WAGNER

WHEN I WAS a little kid, family vacations meant packing six people and all their gear into and on top of a station wagon, then driving eight hours to spend a week in a rustic rental house on the beach. My father judiciously recorded these trips with his 8 mm movie camera, always starting with a prolonged view of the date and place drawn into the sand. He didn't etch those details into a dry patch; he drew them into the wet sand at the water's edge. And he would then film them slowly getting erased by the tidewater.

The Beauty of Wet Sand

I love wet sand. It makes the best sandcastles, with deep moats to keep your brother's armies out. It has a marvelous soft-hard sensation underfoot. And it is a great place to write messages that are not meant to be permanent, like the ones meant for your siblings' eyes but not your parents'.

Wet sand is also an appropriate way to think about how to inspire harmony in corporate governance. To get off on the right foot with your CEO and her management team, a line must be drawn between board roles and management roles, but that line must not be etched in cement. It should be a bright line that everyone can see but that can change as needed; that line is the starting point for concinnity in corporate governance.

Imperative 1 in building a framework for concinnity in corporate governance is to draw the right line between what you as a board member do and what your CEO does as management. As the first thing to get right, it is also one of the most common things boards and CEOs get wrong—together.

Drawing the Line Together

Govern. Rule. Rules. What do these words mean to you? Leadership is about management's activities. Governance is about the board's activities. But what exactly does that mean? Good governance requires having a bright, well-understood line between the two, and it drives business performance in profound ways. How profound? My all-time best and worst client had both inadequate leadership and poor governance. The company was a great client from the standpoint that all of that inadequacy required considerable consulting time on my firm's part. It was my worst because the board's poor governance made it extremely difficult to help them, and the company almost failed.

In my role as a trusted advisor, I have heard board members and management from the same company describe the same situation with completely different perspectives and radically different interpretations. I have heard a former private equity client complain that CEOs don't know how to involve board members. Hearing about my new venture in leadership and governance advisory, she enthusiastically said, "Oh, Nancy, talk about how you can teach CEOs to work better with their boards. So many of them just don't know how to work with us." From her perspective, CEOs—especially in newly acquired portfolio companies—often fail to reach out for advice and counsel, and when boards reach in to help, they resist.

> Leadership is about management's activities.
> Governance is about the board's activities.

I once received a call from a consultant whose client CEO had complained that his board members "were driving him crazy." Not only were they calling him all of the time, asking questions and giving advice, they were not carrying their share of the load on matters of importance to the company. From his perspective, the board didn't know how to work with him.

They were both right. For each of them, the other party was a source of frustration, with too much intervention in some areas and too little help in others. This is what happens when there is not a shared understanding of the dividing line between what the board does and what the CEO does. Acquisition agreements don't come with a manual for how to work together, and for many companies not only is the board entirely new, but the presence of a professional board itself is new. It's no wonder the two parties don't know how to work together.

Half of the time, someone crosses a line that exists in the other person's head, and this drives that person nuts. The other half of the time someone is so afraid of crossing an unclear line, that she will stay so far away from it that she doesn't contribute enough. Both problems result from boards and CEOs failing to examine, define, and refine their respective roles and responsibilities in corporate governance *together*.

There are a few reasons for this. Part of the problem is that many people think working relationships should come naturally to boards and leadership teams—which they don't. Another part of it is that conversations about these roles and responsibilities touch emotional nerves. Still another part is that people wait until multiple problems arise, when considerable frustration discourages dialogue. And then there is that definitional problem.

Board members who see their role as controlling and directing, as opposed to guiding and helping, kindle understandable resistance from CEOs. Then again, board members (I see this a lot in the private equity world) who think they are too busy helping their companies grow to be bothered with the "administrivia" of corporate governance often miss the opportunity to get concurrence on just how much help is helpful. In family-owned companies, a fierce sense of ownership often leads to strong feelings that the clan doesn't need outsiders—who don't have skin in the game—telling them what to do. I have seen this attitude in the venture capital and middle-market private equity worlds, too. It means that they miss out on different perspectives that can only come from the outside, or operational insight that can only come from the CEO or managers on the inside, and they create confusion with management as to proper roles.

Yes, the definitional problem in corporate governance gets in the way, and resistance to addressing corporate governance is a barrier to drawing the right lines the right way—in wet sand.

That Which Lies on Your Side of the Line

> Good fences make good neighbors. —ROBERT FROST

Undoubtedly the line between what management does and what the board does is different for different companies. But there is some degree of general agreement upon the basics. Below are six things that your board and your CEO must jointly agree are the fundamental responsibilities of the board. They are what I call the Irreducible Minimum when it comes to board roles. These are the table stakes. You cannot do your job without a thorough knowledge of the company. It is a lot of work, especially in the beginning, as a friend of mine found out . . .

He had just joined the board of a public company. I asked him how the first board meeting had gone. He looked at me with an expression of exhaustion and said, "It was a lot of work! There was so much to do to get ready for the board meeting. And we seem to have a lot of calls in between! Two of us were new, and two others had been on the board for years.

"The old-timers had seen the rather extensive credit write-ups on some of the country's largest companies several years in a row. For them, committee prep was largely a process of analyzing one year's worth of numbers and news over that same period. For us newbies, what took them maybe twenty minutes took us like an hour and twenty. We had to learn everything about the business, even if it was a household name. Then we had to familiarize ourselves with the last *five* years of financial performance, in detail! It was a lot of work."

The Irreducible Minimum

1. **KNOW** the company (as well as anyone outside of management): *what* it does, *how* it does it, and *the numbers* that show it.

   a. What does it produce and sell, in all of its lines of business; where does it sell and to whom; what are its key competitive differentiators?

   b. What is the company's strategy and what is the plan for getting there? What landmarks lie along the critical path? What climates, markets, competition, and regulatory environments does it operate in?

   c. What is the basic business model; what makes it profitable? What company financials[4] demonstrate this as well as performance, both over time and relative to peers and competitors?

2. **HELP** the company achieve its goals.

   a. Participate in the development of company strategy.

   b. Regularly evaluate progress on growth, profitability, mission expansion, and other goals.

3. **ENSURE** that the company meets its obligations to all stakeholders.

4. **PARTICIPATE** in policymaking and oversight.

5. **REVIEW** and challenge management performance.

   a. Ask the hard questions.

   b. Know senior leadership.

6. **CONTRIBUTE** effectively and constructively to the work of the board.

   a. Be prepared for board meetings.

   b. Ask the right (hard) questions.

   c. Participate in board self-evaluation.

---

4   This includes the financials, in depth, even if you are not a finance jock. You should know what it takes to be profitable and financially sound.

> **THE DUTY OF CARE** means that a director must stay informed, pay attention, and exercise reasonable judgment when making decisions on behalf of the corporation. In other words, don't show up at a board meeting ill informed about what's happening in the business or approve various corporate actions that impact the stockholders and assume that you've discharged your duties.[5]

I reminded my friend that completing the advance reading for a planned board meeting is just the starting point for what you owe your CEO, the rest of the board, and other stakeholders in terms of contribution. From a legal responsibility perspective, it is part of your fiduciary duty, which involves duty of care and duty of loyalty. From a practical perspective, it is not possible to help the company meet its goals and take care of all of its shareholders without this knowledge. Realistically you will not have the basis to guide and challenge management on strategy, policy, and performance without it. My friend's most important responsibility in the short term was to be sure that he was on the same page both with the other board members and with the CEO about where he should concentrate his preparation.

> **THE DUTY OF LOYALTY** means the director must put the interests of the corporation ahead of his or her own pecuniary interests. So, if you own a business that will triple in value once you approve a particular corporate action, don't expect the law to sanction the lining of your own pockets at the expense of the stockholders.[5]

....

5   Definitions adapted from Snyder and Reif, *Answering the Call: Understanding the Duties, Risks, and Rewards of Corporate Governance.*

Once you and your CEO agree on these basics, you can start the process of outlining specifically what you will do with all of that knowledge. Beyond this list is where the fun and challenge begin in crafting a list of board responsibilities customized to your particular company's needs.

The list of possibilities is almost endless. Regardless of your company's size or ownership structure, it is constructive to know and think about the governance standards set for the largest of companies and for public companies.

As Goes Wall Street, So Goes Main Street

From a governance standpoint, as goes Wall Street, so goes Main Street. Said another way, as go the governance standards for publicly traded companies, so go the standards for all other firms—eventually. When I talk with private company board members, they comment on how crazy and unrewarding it would be to be in a governance role in a public company: to be burdened with all those regulatory requirements, from the SEC on down. True, there are significant differences in governance between public and private companies. The line between board and management responsibilities, while different for every company, tends to fall in one range for public companies and quite a different range for private companies. Part of that is ownership, but part of that is size. Nevertheless, the principles of good governance remain the same: Management operates; boards guide. And the trends in governance that have kept public company boards up at night—cyber risk, executive compensation, and board composition, to name a few—are increasingly issues for private companies as well, because concerning oneself with these issues is just good business, no matter how big the enterprise.

During the advent of Sarbanes-Oxley (SOX), I was an officer of a public company. Not long after, I left to join a large private institution in a CFO role. *Whew! Bullet dodged*—or so I thought. Within two years we were considering how to incorporate elements of SOX best practices into our organization, not because we had to, but because it was good business. Separation of duties and documentation of them, one of SOX's main concerns, is good business; good risk management is good for all stakeholders. Public company reporting requirements for board member qualifications is not just an exercise in record keeping; it's good business. These are the kinds of good governance details that can make the difference between whether companies struggle or thrive. Wall Street and Main Street are starting to look more alike, and it's important that you look out the window occasionally and notice when the view starts to seem familiar.

Companies need directors who contribute uniquely and completely in ways the company needs now. Consider sustainability statements, for example. Required for many public corporations, these address the company's ability to continue its environmental, economic, and social business practices indefinitely. Sustainability statements are not just for the very large corporations; at least, asking, "Just how sustainable are our practices?" is not. It's good business to ask about the sustainability of your supply chain, leadership teams, other supplies of human capital, business processes, and systems. Success depends on knowing if these components on which your company relies to survive and thrive can withstand external forces of change, and provide the engines for sustained growth in earnings. The trend toward sustainability reporting may have had its origins in the environmental movement, but it has brought great value to forward-thinking leaders. Environmental policies and plans are not only for the big companies, the risky businesses, the good corporate souls, or organizations with environmentalist constituencies—not any more. If fluctuations in energy prices and talent availability challenges have not hit you lately, I want to know under what rock you are conducting your business; I could sell tickets to everybody who'd want to crawl under it with you.

Most sustainability factors should be elements of good enterprise risk management (ERM), which is not only for the flush corporations that can hire the big consultants. It does seem that companies with complex logistics stay ahead of many in terms of certain sustainability risks, such as weather and climate change, but they affect everyone. An investment banker recently told me how the bad winter was hurting his ability to get deals done; no one could fly to the meetings! Our own office is not immune, either. After a major nor'easter hit the Boston-Washington corridor, our office phones in Nashville went out. Turns out we had trunk lines that went through New York, a fact that had not on been anybody's radar—but should have been. At a recent National Association of Corporate Directors (NACD) presentation on climate risk, a presenter told the audience that if their board didn't have a climate risk policy, they should develop one—as soon as they returned to the office. After his stories of crisis, no one in the audience felt that climate risk was just for those with complex supply chains. By now many of us realize we are in this together when it comes to natural disasters.

The good news is that companies of all sizes and ownership structures can learn from the early adopters: in this case, the large, public companies. We can learn from their mistakes and from their best practices, which undoubtedly demonstrate next steps for companies of all shapes, sizes, and ownership forms.

The trick is to resist the tendency to perceive governance trends and practices as overreaching bureaucracy to be avoided at all costs. Instead, learn to see them as a fully customizable roadmap available to you, your board, and your leadership. Rightsize the programs and processes for your business. My last firm did this by offering our clients a tool to help small-cap public companies rapidly implement a sustainable SOX compliance program. We called it Rapid SOX; some called it SOX Lite. Our clients called it a godsend. We rightsized best practices for each client. It was good business.

Other large-scale governance practices can be rightsized to benefit Main Street. Most boards have, at a minimum, an audit committee, a governance committee, and a compensation committee. While non-fiduciary boards[6] generally have more limited roles—especially regarding the compensation, hiring, and firing decisions handled by compensation committees—even these boards can be of immense value in helping build robust and sustainable leadership teams, and improved human resources cultures and processes. With the ascendancy of corporate risks in general and cyber risk in particular, many companies are adding board risk management if not information technology committees, or at least adding these two things as topics for consideration for the whole board or for board committees. This is yet another governance trend in corporate America that will have value in certain smaller companies, once

6 Non-fiduciary boards include advisory boards, honorary councils and boards, professional councils, and the like. While they provide valuable advice and guidance to management or sometimes even to fiduciary boards, they have neither the responsibilities nor authority of fiduciary boards.

rightsized. These complicated issues require board and management time and attention.

Where to Put Your Nose—and Other Body Parts

Let's return to how to divide up the work. Board members are expected to bring their specific areas of expertise to the table. What they do with them while there depends on what resources the company has internally and upon a shared understanding of roles and responsibilities. Small company board members should expect to roll up their sleeves, but only with consensus around the board and into the C-suite about how to do it and how far to go. Public company directors carry a liability so great it almost ensures they don't become too involved in operations.

Corporate governance circles use the acronym NIFO: Nose In, Fingers Out. It became something of a rule in the largest companies and was designed to help board directors avoid the temptation to get too involved in company operations. No wonder, given the number of seated CEOs on big company boards—what they do best is put their nose, at the minimum, into company operations. A friend of mine who places CEOs talks about the number of execs who come to him as they near retirement age, hoping for help getting on corporate boards. He counsels most of them against it. Why? Because they like to *run* things—not only sticking their noses in, but other body parts as well—and he tells them that the areas where they excel are not what corporate boards are supposed to be doing. Possibly they could be effective in small companies, where those other body parts are more welcome.

Those smaller, often early-stage companies benefit from

what is referred to as a NIEI, or Nose In, Elbows In approach. This group includes most venture capitalists and some private equity sponsors, depending on the portfolio company. For such companies it's all hands on deck, doing whatever they can to add value to the company. I am on the board of a startup health-care company, and what I do there is quite different from my role at the boardroom table of an educational institution that's 150-plus years old. And the pre-IPO (initial public offering) company I am involved with is somewhere in between. They pick their board members to complement gaps in the leadership team. Large, mature companies have internal resources that smaller, early-stage companies don't have, so board members can and must add critical core competencies. These companies are looking for elbows in.

But whether it's fingers out or elbows in, public company or private, it is imperative that you and the CEO decide together the specific roles and responsibilities you each have, as there is still a long list of possible areas for board involvement. How do you get a handle on the right areas of involvement for your board? You talk about it—a lot. Corporate Concinnity is all about consensus and harmony, and it starts with communication. Given the experience that sits around most boardroom tables, there are many points of view. All must be considered.

All the Views Across the Line

I remember a "conversation" my late husband and I had years ago about some problem with the 150-year-old New England colonial home that we were renovating. I could not believe his point of view was so far afield from my own. Expressing his own frustration, he blurted out, "What you want is a twin of yourself!" He

Typical Large Company Governance Sharing

Management Responsibilities — S H A R E D — Board Responsibilities

Typical Small Company Governance Sharing

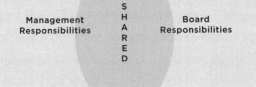

Management Responsibilities — S H A R E D — Board Responsibilities

was almost right. The fault was in my assumption that I did have a twin in thinking on the particular issue we were discussing.

It's easy for any of us to make presumptions about concurrence with close associates, especially when we find ourselves simpatico in thinking much of the time. Communication is key;

you can never have too much dialogue about the ever-evolving nature of what boards should and should not do. Being deliberate about sharing points of view is a critical step in navigating management-board relations.

Have you thought about your point of view lately? Could you articulate it to your board colleagues or your CEO? If you haven't done this recently, you should. The reality is that they have a point of view, too, and if you haven't heard theirs lately, you could be less aligned than you think you are.

How is your view different? As an advisor to boards and CEOs and a mentor to C-suite executives, I have lived in between the partners in the governance/leadership dance. How is my view different from that of my fellow board members? From the CEO's? I am a company-operating executive; I have the perspective of the finance chief. I have the perspective of human capital management, of private equity. I know investor relations. I know capital markets. This makes my view different. It does not make it better.

What is your strongly held view? Do you and your CEO have a shared view of the line between leadership and governance? Have you had a conversation about it? It is crucial to understand your own view, how it may differ from your colleagues', *and* how your view will be seen by board colleagues. Consider how it will be viewed by your CEO and others in the C-suite, on the other side of the governance-leadership line.

Your dialogue should include the differences of ownership: who owns the company and how this impacts what they want. You should discuss the implications of the company's size. The resources that large companies have mean that the board does not get involved in day-to-day operations. With smaller companies, however, limited resources mean the board is often called to participate in activities that in a more richly resourced company would be done by management. Examples include helping with sales and marketing. In larger companies the board may be asked to facilitate introductions but not get involved in the details of sales.

Company size makes a huge difference, and so does ownership structure. A public company, especially a large one, will spend considerably more time on financial and governance regulatory matters, as well as on the concerns of increasingly active shareholders. In small-cap public companies, the smaller and often lower-profile shareholder base can limit the time required to attend to shareholder matters. In private companies, because of the absence of SEC regulatory matters, boards will spend more time on operational strategies. If the private company is private-equity owned, the board may take a very active role in operational activities of a financial nature.

Building concinnity in shared governance is jet-fueled by view awareness and communication. These things are important to your CEO, and they are marvelous table settings for the work you have to do. Working well as a team won't just happen, and it will take more than just practice. It also requires good listening, self-awareness, the ability to learn and be coached, and the capacity to hear advice about things you cannot see—and then the discipline to put the advice into action, just as my daughter used to do at diving practice. She would come up after a dive and listen, while still in the water, to her coach's advice on some finer point of her launch, her rotation, or her leg position. She would go back to the board and execute exactly as he had instructed. She would listen, she would hear and comprehend, and then she would act. All critical elements.

Now Just Show Up

I had a boss several years ago who was fond of saying, "Ninety-five percent of it is just showing up." For years after, I often thought, *That is totally wrong. Just showing up is not it at all; one must be completely engaged.* The problem is that too many people *just* show up. They are not tuned in, not engaged. Concinnity cannot blossom without engagement.

Reading Eknath Easwaran's book *Take Your Time*, one of my all-time favorite books, solidified that belief. He teaches "one-pointed attention," a technique used to create more peace in your life. It does more than that; I have found that one-pointed attention allows me to become virtually locked in on people with whom I am meeting in a mind-meld kind of way. It is an extraordinary gift to the people you are with and can practically turbo-charge relationships. And concinnity in corporate governance is all about relationships that are amazing—in a good way!

We owe our colleagues on the board and in the C-suite the benefit of our full engagement. Yet people often "check out" in leadership meetings. It can also happen in board meetings. Easwaran talks about the high compliment it is to another individual to give your complete, undivided, one-pointed attention. We've all been victims of distracted attention: the networking event where the person to whom you are speaking is regularly looking over your shoulder, the person at the table who is always looking at the smartphone in her lap. It is so common we almost don't even take offense anymore.

With the standard of performance for email response time dropping to under an hour, who *can* afford to ignore the smartphone in her lap? But powerful tools for efficiency—like technology and social media—can also drain us of intention and full engagement with their tendency to reduce our ability to be in the here and now with the people in front of us or with the task at hand. They can keep us from fully showing up. A distracted brain misses a lot. The effective use of one-pointed, fully engaged attention is one of the best tools in an executive's kit. It takes the efficiency of the current meeting, project, or task up about a thousand percent.

Setting intentions also helps engagement. While not every meeting requires tremendous prep, all meetings—including board meetings—require setting your intention in advance. Good agendas help, but as a board member you must set your own intention. How will you help the CEO? How will you carry out your basic duties during this meeting? Your intention, once set, is a fantastic tool for focusing attention, for keeping you present and truly engaged. And it is contagious; it will do the same thing for your colleagues, increasing their efficiency as well. Because of your engagement, your associates, especially your CEO, are first flattered and then equally engaged. Team productivity rises. By the way, so does fun.

I have to consider the possibility that when my old boss said "Just show up," he might actually have meant be engaged. So I am modifying his adage: We need to fully show up! Engagement means hearing what we need to hear and getting done what we must get done with far more efficiency and enjoyment. Don't just show up—*fully* show up. It will change your productivity and the quality of the relationships in your governance work.

Remember the New Normal

Some time ago I herniated a disc in my neck. Labor pains were nothing compared to the pain of that injury! But as with becoming a parent, there were positives and lessons to be learned from the pain. After weeks of stronger-than-I-like-to-take meds, physical therapy, and very limited activity, the pain subsided, but my physical activities were limited. My physical therapist started talking about my finding a *new normal* as it applied to my sitting, standing, and just about everything else. While I felt too young to have to be dealing with real neck issues, I felt too old to need a *new normal*. But that's the way it was.

In business and in governance, new normals are also a constant reality, especially in the corporate arena. Some of us felt that we'd only just put Sarbanes-Oxley to bed in terms of operationally integrating its mandates, when along came Dodd-Frank. And that's just the regulatory side of things. Activist investors are changing the face of governance so drastically that companies, both public and private, have had to rethink how they handle investor relations. And board members must reconsider how much of this activity lies on their side of the line.

While organizations like the National Association of Corporate Directors help directors stay on top of the myriad of issues, boards must still figure out how to respond in a "right-sized" way to new regulations, evolving standards, and changes in the environments in which they operate. There are plenty of boards that, as a whole, prefer to keep their heads in the sand on these issues, and others that are so focused on governance protocol that they lose sight of the main thing, which is ensuring the success of the company while meeting its goals and obligations.

The best boards have a shared philosophy of governance that includes strategies for responding to changes. Together they build the new normal that will allow them to focus on helping management achieve the company's goals, define strategy, establish policy, and be accountable, all in the context of meeting obligations to all stakeholders. They do this on an ongoing basis.

If good corporate governance is a framework through which people, processes, and systems work together to support companies in the achievement of their goals, while simultaneously meeting all their obligations, then boards must be thoughtful and deliberate in finding the new normal in the areas of people, processes, and systems. Again, let's consider risk management as an example. Who should be responsible for it? Many are calling for the oversight of risk management to step outside the confines of the audit committee, where it has typically lived, and be made into its own committee. Others believe risk oversight is a matter for the entire board. Still others call for risk management and oversight to be an element of each board committee's work. Boards must find the right people and processes to ensure proper oversight of this area. New systems will need to be developed to track goals, metrics, and performance. And quite possibly new players, such as board members with the appropriate risk management backgrounds, will need to be identified to help. A new normal must be built for this critical issue, again and again.

Sand, Fences, and Bridges

Fences and lines in the sand suggest separation, but in the context of concinnity in governing, they are really fundamental to building bridges. Making distinctions between what you as a director do and what your CEO does allows you to contribute materially and instrumentally to helping your company meet its goals. Remember to appreciate that the line will move, just like writing in wet sand. Stay committed to continuous dialogue with the CEO to ensure clarity around roles and responsibilities over time. If you do these things, you have taken the first step, the first imperative required to create harmony in putting together the pieces and parts of the governance game. Now let's talk about creating harmony and functionality on the board itself. Getting that right is Imperative 2 in creating concinnity in corporate governance.

A New Framework for Governing

#1 Draw a Line in the Sand

#2 Don't Go Overboard

#3 Assemble at the Same Starting Blocks

#4 Mind the Stakeholder Gap

#5 Manage Your Information Appetite

#6 Be Prepared: Culture and Change Readiness

#7 Don't Leave Compensation to the Experts

#8 Bench Your Inner Coach

#9 Off-Board Well

#10 Cultivate Wisdom

Don't Go Overboard

Moderation in all things, especially moderation.
—RALPH WALDO EMERSON

YOU KNOW THE story: One of the chairs was too big; one was too small. But one was juuuuuust right. In order to achieve concinnity in corporate governance, you must get your board juuuuuust right.

Goldilocks and Governance

Like Goldilocks, you are looking for the best fit in terms of size, composition, and structure. Just as good working relationships depend on establishing clarity on the roles and responsibilities of CEOs vs. boards, it is critical to seat the right players around the boardroom table, to create a structure that will limit conflict without reducing honest dialogue, and to agree on a focus and values that will create harmony. It is easy to go overboard in one direction or another when trying to manage board size, membership, and playbook. I've seen companies repeat the same mistakes over and over again, creating the perfect conditions for conflict. Here are my "favorite" board missteps:

Ten Common Board Mistakes

1. Having too many board members

2. Having too few board members

3. Neglecting to appoint independent directors

4. Misunderstanding representative democracy

5. Having the wrong management representation

6. Failing to get adequate capital markets expertise

7. Maintaining too little diversity

8. Allowing excessive director tenure

9. Failing to establish adequate structure

10. Failing to create a culture of mutual trust, respect, and commitment to concinnity in corporate governance

Size Does Matter

Depending on the organization, some boards are way too big, some are not large enough, and some are just right. When it comes to boards, size matters. The board needs to be rightsized for your company, its stage, and its future plans. Some companies try to keep their boards small in order to contain directors' fees, but that's missing the big picture. (Managing fees should not be a top-five determinant of board size.) Others, especially the not-for-profits that consider their boards largely fundraising organizations, have a "best when bigger" philosophy. Both of these approaches to rightsizing a board are fraught with peril.

Let's start with what I call "the mother of all boards," in terms of size: boards of very large not-for-profit[7] companies. These organizations often have boards somewhere north of fifteen directors; many are double that. These large not-for-profits are big business in this country, dominating industries such as healthcare and education.[8] It would be a mistake to overlook the governance issues in such a large a part of the economy.

While these companies like to focus conversation on the "M" word (mission), adequately funding their operations is critical to them. As it is said, "no money, no mission." While they may generate a substantial portion of their revenues from operations, donations are material to their bottom lines. In many cases not-for-profits understandably focus on board

....

7   At one time such organizations were referred to as nonprofits. We now refer to them more accurately as not-*for*-profits. They may not all call themselves companies, but, in fact, they are—in many cases, huge businesses.

8   Community- and mission-based hospitals provide a large proportion of the hospital care in this country. In the education space, not-for-profits are the norm.

members who can contribute financially to their organizations. They also focus on having representation from all of the major groups that they define as part of their constituents. The resulting boards can become quite bloated.

While it might seem counterintuitive, the larger the board, the smaller its authority. Not only are these overstuffed boards unwieldy in terms of conducting meetings and getting consensus, it is just not possible for everyone on the board to make a meaningful contribution to the dialogue. In all fairness, these boards are not even considered governing boards by their leadership—and sometimes even by the board itself—but rather as advisory boards. Often the problem is that there is so little authority or contribution on the board side of the management-director divide that there is no real or material role for members. By default, such small or diffuse power at the board level places huge power and authority in the hands of management, putting both the organization and its execs in a position of great potential risk. One of the board responsibilities in my "Irreducible Minimum" duties list—challenging management—is extremely difficult to do on these boards.

In addition, board members can really lose the sense of their individual responsibility on these super-sized boards, with so many other capable, often high-level, board colleagues. Partly this is human nature, but part of it is the confusion about individual responsibility around such a large table. The sad reality is that often in an oversized board, any one board member becomes pretty expendable. This presents a real formula for board member apathy, if not impotence.

If a board must be that large—and I personally question this—committee structure is key. Not only must committee roles and responsibilities be very specific, they must also be well understood by the entire board so that, as a whole, the board feels that all key elements of good governance are covered. It is also critical to have a shared understanding of exactly what level of knowledge and questioning non-committee board members should utilize in order to satisfy themselves that the "hard questions are being asked" (one of the most important table stakes), that the questions are being answered by the right people, and also that management is accountable. Good governance is possible in large boards, but it is hard. Well-conceived committee structure and communication are critical, and a CEO who believes in shared governance and in an open door to the organization's senior leadership is key.

All in the Family

Family businesses, too, can fall into the "more is better" trap and end up with boards that are ineffectual at decision making and fertile ground for conflict. For some reason, in their infancy, family boards feel more comfortable with town-hall-meeting–style democracy, as opposed to representative democracy: everyone gets to have a voice.

A friend of mine consults extensively with family businesses, including advising them on corporate governance matters. He was helping a particular three-generation family business to evaluate their board composition, including introducing new thinking in the form of outside, independent directors. The board had become so large that decision making was unproductive, so they wanted to consider reducing the number of directors. However, they were stuck on having representation from each branch of the family, which amounted to a large board even before outside members were brought on. They had become very comfortable with town-hall-style meetings—every stakeholder having a voice—but had lost sight of the fact that it was possible for fewer family members to represent shareholders as a group. If you think about it, that's what board members of large and small public companies do every day. Professional governance cannot begin without informed, high-integrity, representative democracy as an element of stakeholder representation. My friend was able to help his client see and to understand that the point was to represent the family as a whole, not the individual branches, as well as other stakeholders in the company.

Venture and Private Equity Backing: Not Your Average Shareholders

Another friend of mine operates exclusively in the family-owned business space. In sharing experiences, we have become convinced of the similarities between companies owned by families and those owned by venture capital and private equity, when the latter have arrived at the point when outside directors are needed but have not yet been placed—or even sought. From a governance perspective, such firms often think like family-owned companies.

Venture capital–backed or private equity–owned companies have some of the smartest people in the business in their shareholder group: "smart money," they are called, because of their historical returns. They know the industry, are skilled at picking CEO winners (often backing the same teams in serial endeavors), and they rock at financial wizardry. A good number of them, often the largest players in this arena, have become quite good at corporate governance, if not even Corporate Concinnity. But the vast majority of venture capital and private equity players are not the deca-billion-dollar crowd. A significant percentage of American companies are owned by mid-sized private capital players. So, like the very large not-for-profits, it is important to consider them in the corporate governance dialogue. These folks are as new to professional governance as many family businesses are.

These ownership groups figure they are small enough in number that it is easy to put everyone on the board, give everyone a voice. Sounds logical, right? If you have arrived at the point of being ready for independent directors, so the reasoning goes, you need to have enough shareholders on the board to balance the votes of the non-owners. In reality, as with many family-owned businesses, these groups are also stuck in town-hall-meeting–style democracy and missing the point of representation. But one share/one seat does not reduce chances for conflict, nor does it lead to better or easier governance.

I had a client who was funded by what is called a private equity "club deal": financing provided by a small group of venture or private equity groups. Each private equity group put up the same amount of money, so each group got a seat on the board. There were no independent board members. There was one former owner group, represented by an "observer" on the board who brought institutional memory and subject matter expertise, but his was a non-voting role. Well, the company got into some trouble and needed a turnaround in short order. Tough decisions were required, quickly. More capital was also needed. Unfortunately the four people with equal voting power had different opinions about what was needed to save the company. And each had a different appetite for additional investment and risk. Each one of them, focused on his own shareholders or optimizing her own relative investment, had lost sight of representing all shareholders. With no other stakeholders at the table, even virtually, fiduciary care—the duty of loyalty, of putting the corporation's interests above one's own—seemed to be out the window.

So many well-intended private capital investors think they are taking the greatest care of their investment by adhering to a one share/one vote structure. However, they miss out on the wisdom of independent directors and the brilliance of representative democracy when it comes to good corporate governance. From the get-go, these boards are structured for internal warfare, as opposed to framed for concinnity in corporate governance.

I have found that small- and mid-sized private equity groups fall into two categories: those that value independent directors, and those that don't. Many firms value outside directors in concept, but haven't figured out how to make the transition. I hope that the lessons in this book will help them get there.

A board can be too large, giving staff and management too much control. It can also be too small, limiting the kind of independent and new thinking that outside directors offer. Outside directors bring new input to the table that offers invaluable context to the hyper-focused financial interest of some other board members. In both cases, matters are aggravated by equal shares representation being the alpha and the omega, and board size making it difficult to define members' roles. Size matters; your board must be just big enough to provide the depth and breadth of leadership that your company needs, right now.

Quality Trumps Quantity

Size does matter, but the most important factor in determining board size is not the size at all. Instead, the most critical task is determining what skills, experiences, and contributions you need on your board. The board is there to help the company achieve its mission and goals while balancing responsibilities to a variety of stakeholders. Where is the company trying to go? What resources on a board would help it get there? The relationship between the CEO and the board is a key partnership, and the directors' experiences and skills should complement the CEO's.

A "board expertise" matrix is the best place to start in determining the expertise you need to harness. There are plenty of versions out there, but a pretty simple spreadsheet detailing "must have" and "nice to have" competencies and backgrounds is a fine place to start. Below are two sample board skills matrices. Use the first to summarize the skill sets of current board members. This matrix uses basic (B), intermediate (I), and expert (E) levels of expertise for each board member's skill or experience set. The completed matrix will provide a picture of what strengths and needs exist for the board. The second matrix should be used to quantify the same skill sets over time to see what changes as board members change. Each cell in this matrix is calculated as follows: skill rating equals number of directors with basic skills in this area multiplied by one, plus the number of directors with intermediate skill multiplied by two, plus the number of directors with advanced skill by 3.

Board Skills Matrix

KNOWLEDGE/ EXPERTISE/ CATEGORY	SPECIFIC EXPERTISE BY BOARD MEMBER						
Functional Skills	1	2	3	4	5	6	7
Financial Expertise							
Industry Expertise							
International Expertise							
Regulatory/Government							
Technology							
Risk Expertise							
Marketing							
Digital or Social Media							
Strategic Planning							
Comp Expertise							
Banking							
Capital Formation							
Capital Markets							
Workout & Turnaround							
Change Agent							
Talent Management/HR							
Core Competencies							
Visionary							
Connector							
Strategic Thinker							
Accountability							
Organizational Learning							
Board Tenure							
Term End							
Other Critical Criteria							
Business Development							
Audit Comm. Financial Expert							
Diversity							
Independence							
Investor Relations							
Governance							

B=Basic   I=Intermediate   E=Expert

Board Skills Matrix

KNOWLEDGE/ EXPERTISE/ CATEGORY	DEPTH OF EXPERTISE BY YEAR						
Functional Skills	Current	2	3	4	5	6	7
Financial Expertise							
Industry Expertise							
International Expertise							
Regulatory/Government							
Technology							
Risk Expertise							
Marketing							
Digital or Social Media							
Strategic Planning							
Comp Expertise							
Banking							
Capital Formation							
Capital Markets							
Workout & Turnaround							
Change Agent							
Talent Management/HR							
Core Competencies							
Visionary							
Connector							
Strategic Thinker							
Accountability							
Organizational Learning							
Board Tenure							
Term End							
Other Critical Criteria							
Business Development							
Audit Comm. Financial Expert							
Diversity							
Independence							
Investor Relations							
Governance							

B=1   I=2   E=3   (multiply times number of board members)

The must-have skill sets will often include such things as financial acumen, industry knowledge, and experience building and running businesses. From there on, lists include entrepreneurial capability, IT savvy, regulatory experience, investor relation skills, international contacts and knowledge, M & A proficiency, marketing know-how, and operational expertise and experience. It is best to start out with an ambitious wish list. You can always prune it back, but you will most certainly find that many great board directors and director candidates meet multiple criteria on such a list. So think big (in terms of needs, not size!). Thoughtful consideration should be given to the issue of diversity of ideas, if not demographics. At a minimum, you want your board to be representative of your customer base and perhaps of your key stakeholders. But be careful here; wanting to have "complete representation" can be a trap, as discussed earlier, especially for large not-for-profit and family-owned businesses.

It is also critical to think about your company's age and life stage. If you are early-stage, someone with entrepreneurial experience would be helpful for your board. But what's most important to consider is where the company is headed. What challenges will the next few years present? You will want to consider having on the board people who've succeeded in business at a similar stage with similar challenges and opportunities. What are the critical success factors for the company over the next several years? If your growth requires changes or augmentation on the talent side, that could be a must-have board member skill. If you plan to raise debt or equity, capital markets expertise could be critical. In fact, that's an often under-represented competency, especially in companies that need it most: small- and micro-cap companies.[9]

Like all early-stage and smaller companies, these corporations are severely resource-constrained; they just happen to be public. They often limit the size of their boards to contain costs, to their own disadvantage. Where they don't have the ability to hire full-time expertise, a board member could fill in the gaps. Adam Epstein, in *The Perfect Corporate Board: A Handbook for Mastering the Unique Challenges of Small-Cap Companies*, says this is particularly important in the area of capital markets expertise. Micro-cap companies are constantly seeking additional capital, and yet they are often unable to attract CFOs with the kind of capital markets expertise that large companies can. They may have great operational financial acumen, but capital is not only the lifeblood of these companies, it is extremely expensive. The dollars and "sense" gap between capital solutions that are well crafted and those that are not can be huge. That gap can determine whether a company makes it to the next round or not.

And just in case you think small-cap and micro-cap companies aren't a big part of the corporate picture, consider that well over half of US public companies have market capitalization of less than $300 million (micro-cap). More than 80 percent are small-cap, with market capitalization of less than $2 billion.[10]

....

9   Adam Epstein has written a great book to address the particular needs of the micro-cap public company: *The Perfect Corporate Board: A Handbook for Mastering the Unique Challenges of Small-Cap Companies* (McGraw-Hill, 2012). I recommend it for all leaders, both on boards and in management of small-cap companies.

10   http://www.sec.gov/info/smallbus/acspc/appendi.pdf.

On Diversity

A friend of mine once said to me, "Nancy, never go on a board if their main reason for wanting you is to check a diversity box. It's a surefire setup for being that marginalized board member."

Don't get me wrong; I feel passionate about board diversity. In my own board roles I often bring diversity to the table, but it is not the line with which I lead my own story. I was speaking with an advisor to business owners about my interest in serving in a board capacity for companies he might know. He commented, "How great; there is such a demand for women on boards." First, I reminded him of the difference between need and demand; more companies need them than want them. Then I told him that my own board expertise had less to do with diversity and more to do with financial expertise, experience with building and running businesses, skill in managing human capital, and extensive knowledge of risk management.

He stopped me before I got to the rest of my list, saying, "Point well made." But I told him my Bradlees story, anyway, to make another point.

Bradlees was a publicly traded discount department store chain that operated mainly in the Northeast. If you don't know it, think of a cross between JC Penney and Target.[11] It was the kind of store most men would avoid unless they were very comfortable with their manhood. I was a senior vice president and one of a four-person senior credit committee at a large regional bank, just a stone's throw from a Bradlees location. Bradlees had been an important relationship for the

....
11   I think enough time has passed; the facts speak for themselves or are a matter of public record, so I can tell this story publicly.

bank for a number of years, probably thirty at that point. It consumed a lot of bank services, including credit. Because of the large dollar amount of our credit facility devoted to Bradlees, approval had to come from the credit committee. During my first month or so on the credit committee, the Bradlees deal came up for renewal. The numbers did not look good; the trends were all down. The head of the committee articulated what we were all feeling: "Geez, this doesn't look good. This is a tough one." We had a long history with the company, but the financial conditions had declined to the point where it looked like a much riskier loan than we would like to make. The committee head mused, "I've honestly never even been in a Bradlees store." Then he turned to his right and asked, "John, have you?" John laughed as though he had been asked a ridiculous question and assured us he had not. So he asked the third member if he had—again, no. Still shaking his head while studying the numbers, he finally asked me. As a woman, I had a consumer experience with the store that few men did. I responded, "As a matter of fact, I was there Saturday afternoon." You've never seen three heads swivel faster. I added, "The inventory was a mess, the checkout process cumbersome, the staff clearly didn't know what they were doing. I'll never go back." We turned down the deal. Within a matter of months the company filed for bankruptcy. With that one decision, made possible with the different experience I brought to the table, we dodged a $25 million bullet.

Hearing this, my friend nodded broadly. "Another point well made." Like most men, he would not have been caught dead in a Bradlees store. I brought diversity to the table on this committee. It happened because the committee size had been increased in order to bring in someone with additional, different areas of expertise.

Time to Move On

Many companies feel they are not in a position to grow the size of their boards; thus, they don't know how to find room for diversity. They make the same argument about bringing management onto boards. Were they to look deeper, many would find that they are stuck at a certain size because existing board members have sustained very long tenures.

There are few spheres of life where we are comfortable without term limits. For some reason, corporate governance seems to be one of those spheres. The root cause of this is often found in the biases brought to the table and the necessary role for family or for investors. Thinking about representative democracy avoids this pitfall.

Term limits are a great way to ensure that boards are infused with new ideas and new energy on a regular basis. Director retirement ages are another tool to ensure this. Opponents of term limits argue that the practice creates loss of institutional memory. However, I assert that term limits prevent other board members from failing to do their job of learning that institutional history. In addition to creating space for diversity and management, term limits can reduce director burnout and expand or refresh constituency representation, thereby improving stakeholder trust. Recognizing when it is time for you or one of your directors to move on can do wonders for increasing stakeholder confidence.

Other Director Qualities—the Touchy-Feely Ones

Assuming at this point we are clear on the size and expertise elements conducive to building concinnity in corporate governance, what must we do to get our boards to feel like teams? In the old days, we could just get golf buddies, business pals, and friends from the club to join our boards. We were already a team of sorts, so we just brought that quality to the work of our companies. I think that's how my father got his first independent board position, even though he'd already been on the boards of two companies that he invested in before that and he ran a family business.

In those days, calling on a buddy for board service increased the likelihood that you would add to your board someone you believed had other qualities—the touchy-feely ones—that are so important to building a great board group. However, just reaching out to your buddies is no longer considered best practice; this approach can miss a wealth of talent. But being deliberate about adding directors with those touchy-feely qualities is just as important as it ever was. There are several hard-to-measure but really important qualities you want to find around your boardroom table. Here are my top five:

My Top Five "Other" Qualities

1. Trust

2. Respect

3. Passion for corporate performance

4. Generous listening

5. Playing by the roles and rules

Trust and Respect

In a board setting it is important to like your colleagues, if at all possible. Of course, as Peter Bregman points out about business associates in his book *18 Minutes: Find Your Focus, Master Distraction, and Get the Right Things Done*: "You don't have to like them, you just have to work with them."[12] But you must at least respect them, which is like saying that you have to like aspects of them. You have to respect and appreciate what they bring to the table. It is important to point this out, because I have talked about and seen lots of boards where people didn't necessarily like one another, but they did trust and respect one another. It is important to understand this and keep it in mind.

Passion for Corporate Performance

You want board members who have a passion for corporate performance driven by good leadership and good governance. This is the desire to work in harmony, to build Corporate Concinnity.

Recently, I found myself talking to a friend, justifying a decision to leave a large, national, well-respected advisory firm in order to focus my energies on governance in times of leadership or organizational transitions. "I guess," I said, "I have a real passion for governance." "What?" she exclaimed. "You have just disqualified yourself. Most companies are really just looking for a rubber stamp!"

I laughed. Maybe I was overusing the passion phrase. And certainly, as a woman invading the domain of older, decidedly

....
12   (New York: Business Plus, 2012).

dispassionate males, I needed to avoid communicating the least smidgen of radicalism. So . . . passion? Dial it down, please!

. . . Or should I? It certainly resonates with shareholder activists who are committed to stamping out rubber-stamp boards.

Listening Generously

A good board consists of individuals who each bring something different to the table, something that they can contribute to the work the board must do for the organization—industry knowledge, financial acumen, legal perspective, marketing, the usual suspects. A good board is not a group of clones. The richness of different backgrounds is the solution—as well as the problem.

After all, marketing people don't think like human resources professionals. Lawyers don't think like finance jocks. And entrepreneurs are successful because they don't spend too much time thinking about any of those inside, functional areas. But in the process of becoming, say, a finance jock, one develops some pretty deep-seated biases. Take our pet issue: risk. Less is more for most finance people, unless of course we are talking about significant returns, diversification, and appropriate contingencies, if not hedges. So how do the ideas of the most creative marketing minds get thoroughly heard by the hardcore finance jock? It requires listening with generosity.

What is listening generously?[13] It means listening with the intention of finding value in the speaker's words. You *want* to like the ideas; you *want* to agree. Bregman says that you should

13 Michael Jinkins, *Called to Be Human* (Grand Rapids, MI: William B. Eerdmans Publishing Co., 2009).

listen, hoping to find someone to challenge your own ideas—especially when you think you are right.[14]

Listening generously is difficult because we come to the table with not only our own occupational biases about the right courses of action, we come with biases against and/or about those other disciplines. "Those risk-averse attorneys . . ." "Those sentimental human resources people . . ." "Those bean-counting CFOs . . ."

Biases get in the way of listening generously because before they even speak, we: 1) think we know what they are going to say, and 2) already think they over-think about certain things. But if we work really hard at generous listening, it can make a difference.

Playing by the Roles and Rules

There are other things that help, such as getting to know your board—well. This allows each board member to play by the rules and execute his or her appropriate role. Board planning has come full circle, from the days of lavish entertaining (read *Barbarians at the Gate* lately?), to a few decades of austerity, and back again. Hosting board retreats and meetings in a variety of locations is now in vogue again. This time around, however, it's not so much about lavishing perks on your board as it might have been thirty years ago. Nowadays, it's more about getting folks away from the workaday hustle and bustle so they have an opportunity to get to know one another.

When I was a young banker my boss told me you could tell a lot about people by they way they golfed. Now that I am again a golfer, I believe that more than ever. Understandably, not everyone is a golfer, but everyone plays at something.

....
14   Bregman, *18 Minutes.*

And you can learn a lot about them by the way they play. Offsite meetings give boards the gift of time to really get to know one another. Once you know about a colleague's family you begin to understand that person significantly better. Once you appreciate that he or she is active in the sandwich generation stage of life, struggling with teenage angst and elderly dementia in the people they love most, you begin to have compassion.

I had the opportunity to join a new board that was formed to direct a new organization. It was an interesting case study in how to make a board feel like a team, which can happen only when, in addition to the hard, technical skills, you also have these five touchy-feely qualities well instilled in the board as a whole.

I would say that with the exception of a couple of people on the new board, the members were acquainted but did not know each other well, personally or professionally. I think we initially felt that it would be enough to come to the table with a real commitment to the mission of the organization. Not so. We needed to get to know one another much better in order to deepen our mutual trust and respect, to be able to listen generously, and then to fulfill our appropriate roles.

Order and Process

Now that you've determined the right size, composition, and quality elements of your board—the substance, if you will—you need a playbook to bring clarity to the roles and responsibilities of the board itself, for the individual members, and for the committees and chairs. Board rules should be articulated in writing and should be voted upon. All board members must know the rules like the backs of their hands—and when memory doesn't serve, the playbook can. At a minimum your board should have the following governance documents:

1. Bylaws
2. Rules of Order
3. Mission Statement
4. Policies
5. Corporate Charter
6. Committee Charters
7. List of Governing Bodies

You may require more documents, depending on the nature of your organization.

In addition, the board interested in professional governance should have the following operating and process guideline documents:

1. Procedures
2. Roles and Responsibilities
3. Multi-Year Meeting Calendar
4. Meeting Agendas
5. Minutes
6. Board Dashboard

Again, the nature of your business may demand more.

A discussion about board composition and structure would not be complete without mention of the leadership of the board itself. Who's on first? Who runs the show? Who chairs the meetings? Companies, often by virtue of their size, stage of life, or ownership structure, have an established role for the CEO of the company on the board, often including leadership of it.

In family-owned businesses and privately owned companies where the CEO has a majority share of ownership, the CEO often, and usually justifiably, serves as board chair as well. Those CEOs are firmly planted on both sides of the leadership-governance divide by virtue of their role as a major (maybe even majority) shareholder. The best of those chairmen and CEOs understand professional governance, value independent directors, are comfortable with representative democracy, and practice Corporate Concinnity in governance. Others need some help with one or another of these elements. They need to figure out how to calibrate the interests of management, shareholders, and other stakeholders, using the skill of Lady Justice, whose proverbial scales are always balanced.

In SEC-governed companies there has been a trend away from the company CEO serving as chair of the board of directors. The rationale is that a CEO chair is unable to play the role of hiring, evaluating, and holding management accountable when he himself is a part of management. Good governance is all about the harmonious separation of management and governance. CEO chairs straddle both sides of the line. In publicly traded companies where the CEO wears both of these hats, one of the outside directors often serves in such a board leadership role, in the capacity of what is called lead director. The lead director, as a non-management director of a public company who provides leadership to the full board without serving as chair, accommodates the need for separation of roles and responsibilities between management and the board.

Leadership of a board of directors is an immense responsibility. How that leader is determined and the specifics of the role are the subject not only of SEC opinions. They are a very hot topic among shareholders, and not just the activists. And as mentioned earlier, as goes Wall Street, so goes Main Street . . . eventually. So it is one of the composition topics that should be discussed regularly by your board.

> To go to any extreme is to limit oneself. —MARTY RUBIN

The Goldilocks Board

Together, governing documents, rules, processes, and procedures create the basic framework upon which to build Corporate Concinnity in governance. A board that has clarity in its own roles and responsibilities and knows what it should do and should not, can properly set boundaries with the CEO and the leadership team. Setting clear roles for the CEO vis-a-vis the board and building a board with good substance and form so that directors play well as a team ensures that the two sides of the leadership-governance divide are positioned to work together with the kind of clarity that will reduce conflict. The next step is to set about the task of agreeing upon the starting point: Imperative 3 in building Corporate Concinnity in the boardroom.

A New Framework for Governing

#1 Draw a Line in the Sand

#2 Don't Go Overboard

#3 Assemble at the Same Starting Blocks

#4 Mind the Stakeholder Gap

#5 Manage Your Information Appetite

#6 Be Prepared: Culture and Change Readiness

#7 Don't Leave Compensation to the Experts

#8 Bench Your Inner Coach

#9 Off-Board Well

#10 Cultivate Wisdom

Assemble at the Same Starting Blocks

Coming together is a beginning; keeping together is
progress; working together is success. —HENRY FORD

ONE OF MY all time favorite business quotes is from the "Fluff in
my ear" scene in *Winnie the Pooh*, in which Pooh and Piglet are
listening to Rabbit hatch a big plan. But, Pooh has not been paying attention. He asks Rabbit to repeat himself, to which Rabbit
says, "Where do I start from?" The two of them go around and
around, trying to figure out the exact point where Pooh stopped
listening, so that Rabbit knows where to "start from."

The Pooh Problem, or, Where Do I Start From?

I would be willing to swear that I have heard this scene replayed in
both the boardroom and the C-suite among real men and women.
It never ceases to amaze me how many business people have what
I call the Winnie the Pooh Problem: they don't know "where they
are starting from." In the last chapter we talked about assembling
the right people and then establishing consensus on roles and
responsibilities. This is a foundational step in building a framework for Corporate Concinnity. A board must understand its own
role in order to manage the line between what it does and what

management does. It must also be deliberate about evaluating and holding itself accountable for excellence in governance, just as it holds management accountable for company performance.

To do both of these things and to move toward shared goals, it is absolutely critical to know where you are starting from: to put yourselves at the same starting blocks. It is also critical for new owners, be they strategic or financial buyers, to understand exactly what they bought. There are an infinite number of possible starting points, which is perhaps why there is so much confusion about exactly where it is for a given company. Here are some typical examples:

Typical Company Stages and Starting Points

1. Concept stage

2. Proof of concept stage

3. Revenue/Infrastructure Scaling

4. Organic growth

5. Acquisition

6. Transformation

7. Turnaround

8. Recovery

9. Wind down

10. Breakup, sell-off

This list is far from inclusive. And it may seem overly basic or pedantic to categorize business stages in as detailed or systematic a way as this. You may think it obvious for a newly acquired company or division to think this through, but it may not occur to you that every board ought to examine the starting point for the company each and every year, at a minimum. Agreeing on the starting point means that you have a reasonable chance at agreeing to what is needed to get to the next point. You must also agree upon the next point. If you don't have rock-solid agreement on this, your chances of getting where you want to go eventually are slim. In addition, tremendous forces in the market, as well as regulatory, social, and economic environments, change businesses in fundamental ways and at astonishing rates. It is critical to constantly ask the question, "Where do we start from?" And it is absolutely necessary for everyone around the boardroom table to agree upon the starting point.

Starting and Restarting, with Regularity

I have a strong memory of a community hospital board. We were there because the hospital was failing, and we had been asked to submit a proposal on providing an entirely new leadership team to turn the hospital around. We had our first meeting with the entire board. My colleague began: "Could we go around the room and have all of you answer the question, 'What is your vision for this hospital?'" They were more than willing to do that.

This board had all the usual suspects for a community hospital, almost as if each person had come from Central Casting: the retired physician, the pharmacist, the clergyman, the attorney, a few local business people. Each spoke in turn of his vision for the local hospital.

Silly me, I was expecting to hear thoughts about rationalizing lines of services in order to stay in business. After all, we were there to turn the hospital around. But, no . . . nary a voice of rationalization came from the boardroom table. There were echoes of support for focus on the typical critical lines of business: the emergency department and obstetrics, among others. But several individuals expressed the opinion that the hospital should never become anything less than a full-service hospital. Some even talked about how important it was for the hospital to *reclaim* lost lines of services. In their minds, the hospital needed to be returned to its former glory. The talk was expansive—visionary, even.

One person at the table, however, was neither expansive nor expressive of great things for the future. There were several lively monologues, but this gentleman did not participate. He spent the entire exercise sitting silently to my left. To me, it appeared that this man was sweating—profusely—for the entire meeting. We thought him quite odd at first, but then we figured it out. He was the controller of the hospital. He watched the dollars and cents—daily. His problem? He was worried about making payroll . . . tomorrow.

While the governing board of the organization waxed grandiose about a new future, this member of management was worried about the possibility that the very next day the hospital would close due to a shortage of cash for basic daily operations. Not one board member articulated a similar concern. The wildly divergent worries of this one person revealed a profound lack of concinnity.

Talk about a disconnect! These board members were not dancing to the same music at all (and it seemed to us that the controller could hear the band playing a funeral march). It was hard to believe that the board was truly not aware of the hospital's cash flow problems. It is likely that there was information asymmetry, meaning that management knew more about what was going on with the financials than the board. If that was, in fact, the case, they had succeeded in creating a board-management disconnect of company-killing proportions.

This situation was an extreme case; the lengthy discussion about the future and appropriate lines of business to pursue did not resound with agreement and mutual affirmation as each shared his vision. It was almost as though this was either the first time they had had this discussion, or that each time they had it, they never got anywhere close to consensus. No, this board did not work as a team: not with each other, nor with hospital leadership. They were crouched over completely different starting blocks. When the gun sounded, some were ready to race but others were ready to fall dead in their tracks. How on earth were they going to get where they had to go?

This was not a new company for any of the players, so you might want to give them a little grace for not being at consensus on their new starting place, a new destination, and a strategy for getting there. I would like to give them the benefit of assuming they had done such an analysis at some point in the past. But the reality is that the world had changed while the board was not watching. They needed to redefine where they were, where they could go, and how they would make the journey.

One could also argue that mismanagement caused this hospital's crisis. Of course, it played some role. But this was an extreme case of misgovernance. While declining reimbursements were a reality for them, this hospital was in trouble long before healthcare reform set in. Actions on the part of competitors changed their market space. As a result, they were essentially starting over, but they just didn't know it. The board had not taken the time to determine what stage of life the organization was in at that moment in time.

The fact is that over time, the life stages of a business and the major corporate events that accompany them are pretty predictable. When I was running specialty human capital businesses that gave companies on-demand access to C-level executives for projects and seated roles, we often started conversations with a discussion of company stages of life and how each stage required different human capital solutions. If a startup is successful, a company will grow—slowly at first, and then more rapidly. Growth can happen organically, through product or market expansion, or inorganically, through acquisition. At some point growth will require more capital, which will be acquired through new debt or equity, or possibly through an initial public offering (IPO). The chart below shows a sampling of corporate life stages over time.

If your board hasn't recently discussed the company's stage of life and its implications, it would be a good idea to look carefully at this chart, which can help you identify where you are now and where you are headed. Identify your starting point. Where is your company on this graph? What direction and at what pace is your company moving? This information can help a board gather at the same starting line and focus on those resources, talent and otherwise, required to get to your desired destination.

Organizational Transitions

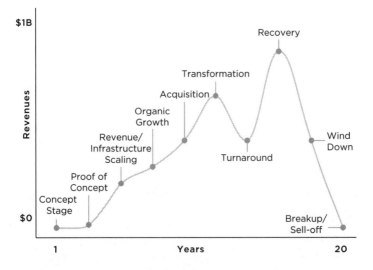

Business cycles, in terms of time, are nothing like they used to be. Take the paper industry, for example. Back in my banking days, its business cycle was predictably seven years long. Part of that was related to the fact that paper companies must plant trees, grow them over a number of years, and harvest them to produce revenue. It was a very predictable and very long business cycle. From the perspective of human capital needs—of skill sets required to manage up and down the business cycles—timing is everything. In that long cycle environment, if an executive was good at growing businesses, but inexperienced at turning them around, he or she had plenty of time to acquire that expertise on the job. Smart people can learn a lot in three and a half years!

Today's executives do not have that luxury. Business cycles today are far shorter than seven years; some are even less than a year. Companies can find themselves out of business overnight, based on the speed of market movement or competitors. The chart below is more representative of today's business cycles:

Business Cycles

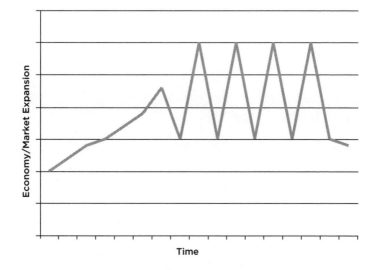

Instead of long, slow curves, the chart shows that today's business cycles look like a graph of shock waves during an earthquake.[15] Even the smartest executive doesn't have the time to learn on the job the way she could have in the past. Compressed timelines have forever changed the nature of managing human capital in business . . . and human capital is not the only resource that has been affected. So, the board must always ask, "What's the starting point, where are we going, and what resources will we need when we get there?" Further, since some stages look alike, the resource requirements can be misunderstood. The board needs to understand this in order to properly fulfill its role.

....

15   http://eqseis.geosc.psu.edu/~cammon/HTML/Classes/IntroQuakes /Notes/waves_and_interior.html.

Where Are We Going?

Getting the right talent for where you are and where you must go is essential. I wrote in the last chapter about the impact of this decision on board composition. Just as important is getting the *board's* collective mind around the current stage and where you are going. This is table stakes for concinnity in corporate governance. It is not possible for teams of directors and leadership to work well together when they don't share the same notion of where they are, where they are going, and how they will get there.

Another company with which I have worked executed a long string of successful acquisitions. Its growth strained the management team, so the C-suite was expanded with talent experienced in making acquisitions and integrating them into current operations—a classic formula for a roll-up play. Since acquisitions require significant capital, companies maneuvering in this fashion must always focus on raising capital to maintain dry powder for making acquisitions. Relying on stock alone is not only insufficient; it is the most expensive way, in weighted-average cost of capital, to fund a company.

So this company needed to tap into the debt market on a consistent basis. The company board generally approved such major strategic and financial activities, as is true for most companies. But when management sought approval for a particular large bond financing, the board was not satisfied that it had a handle on what the funds would be used for. The board did not share management's view and quite possibly did not even have a shared understanding of accessing the debt markets as a strategy of agility in order to optimize value when acquiring companies. Board members were more worried about the company's ability to service the debt than about not having capital to move quickly. They did not see the vision for growth through acquisition, and they turned the financing request down. Not only was it a disappointing moment in history for concinnity in governance, it was also a frustrating moment for management and a defining moment for the company.

It wasn't too long before the window closed on the bond markets—the supply of bond debt financing dried up. As a result, when the management team finally identified suitable acquisitions, it could not secure the debt funding it needed to complete them. At that point, what had been a company on a rapid growth path became a company winding down. An acquisition story became a tale of divestiture in an incredibly short period of time.

It didn't have to turn out that way. The board of the company—you would be surprised at how large it was—may have had a shared understanding of where they were, but it certainly did not agree on how to get from that point to its future self. External forces effectively reset the company's starting point for it.

Growing How?

It is important to know just how your company is or is not growing and what it must do to grow. This requires tremendous ongoing and open-minded evaluation on the part of management and the board. Dick Cross, in his book *The 60-Minute CEO: Mastering Leadership an Hour at a Time*, emphasizes the centrality of thinking as the major element of the CEO's job.[16] I believe much of his advice rings true for a board, as well. Cross outlines a literal back-of-the-envelope technique for focusing thinking on customers' values, wants, and needs. Doing this can create discipline in thinking about your business. His technique, which I highly recommend, is terrific in divining not only where you are starting, but also how you will get where you want to go—or, let's say, where you want to grow. Such devices can help ensure that the board, along with its partners in management—the CEO and the C-suite—get on the same starting blocks, agree on the destination, and gain consensus on how to get there. Regardless of your methodology, your board must get busy thinking about this topic.

> Change happens by listening and then starting a dialogue with the people who are doing something you don't believe is right. —JANE GOODALL

I've had private equity clients who invested in what they thought were growth companies. Once we placed new teams or new leaders in the company, it was clear that what they really had was something altogether different. That was the case for a healthcare supplier, which was acquired as a platform on which to grow through acquisition. The company was to be something of a roll-up strategy based on greater scale and lower costs. In reality, the company turned out to be a bit of a one-trick pony that would have difficulty growing unless it developed a new trick. It was a very competitive space, growth required more speed than was planned for, and that

16   (Brookline, MA: Bibliomotion, 2014).

speed required more capital. As you might imagine, this led to strains between the C-suite and the board. Expectations were based on different assumptions about what it would take to get the company growing. Since there was no way everyone could be right, conflict was guaranteed and disagreements inevitable.

The fact is that once set, our expectations are hard to adjust fully, especially when it requires additional capital! This is not a great place to start building concinnity. But had the board previously engaged in thinking about where the company was and what it would take to grow in a disciplined way, they would have not made this mistake.

Turnaround or Transformation?

If you are not familiar with the three-envelopes joke about management, here it is.

A guy takes over as CEO of a new company. The outgoing CEO hands him three envelopes. He says to him, "Open the first envelope as soon as you get to your new office. After a time—and you will know when—things will not be going as well as you hoped. That is the time to open the second envelope. After another period of time—and again you will know when—things will once more not be going as you hoped. That is when you should open the third envelope."

The new CEO dutifully returns to his office and opens the first envelope. It says, "Blame your predecessor." So the guy does just that. It works like a charm. With this version of historical events, everything that is wrong with the company happened on the CEO's predecessor's watch, leaving him blameless.

After the passage of some time, people no longer want to hear about mistakes made by a former CEO and how that caused all current ills. They become impatient for results. But they are slow in coming. The new CEO figures this means it is time to go back and open the second envelope, so he does just that. It reads, "Reorganize." So that is what he does. And you know what? That advice also works well. Things begin to happen. Progress is made. People seem to be pleased. The changes produce a nice run for the new CEO.

But then, again, it becomes hard to make the numbers. Things aren't going well; people are no longer satisfied. So the CEO goes back to his desk in search of the third envelope. Once he finds it he eagerly rips it open. It reads, "Prepare three envelopes . . ."

While this is a joke, CEOs actually deploy this "technique" all the time. They blame their predecessors, they reorganize, and when they can't make it happen they leave. This happens often because they or their boards cannot tell the difference between a turnaround and a transformation.

I don't recommend deploying the three-envelope method of management, but I do recommend it as a thought exercise. If a CEO can get his or her predecessor to engage in this exercise, then he will learn a tremendous amount about what did and did not work, both during his tenure and before it, in terms of reorganizations and other actions. I do recommend asking, in a half-joking-but-serious way, what the predecessor's three-envelope tactics may have looked like. Said another way: What did the previous leader do that did not work? A predecessor who will speak candidly about what didn't work is worth his or her weight in gold. Finding out about reorganizations that were made and how they were and were not effective will be incredibly helpful.

Certainly, the incoming CEO's experience will probably

be different. The new person no doubt believes he or she will be far more up to the task—which is why the change has been made in the first place. Nonetheless, the candid comments of an outgoing executive can teach you a lot that you wouldn't learn otherwise—maybe even keep you from mistaking a turnaround for a transformation.

A friend of mine was hired to transform a business. He was totally up for the challenge, having previously accomplished it at another company. He had discussed the nature of the company's business, its past, and its vision with people inside and outside the company. The more he talked to people, the more he developed a mental picture of what was needed for the transformation. There seemed to be a shared view of the company's present. All were gathered at the same starting line; they were poised for breakout growth if they could just fix a few things.

The problem was, it wasn't a transformation—it was a turnaround. How did he miss that? Because turnarounds can look like transformations. In the middle of them, we like to convince ourselves—those of us inside the company—that we are just about to reach that breakout point. But it is critical to ask the question, "Is this really a transformation, or is it a turnaround?"

You might be surprised to know that turnarounds can look a lot like transformational opportunities. But there is a subtle yet powerful difference between them. The latter is poised for breakout growth and performance, in short order. The former will suck resources and human energy at a rate you can't imagine. Both transformations and turnarounds can define moments of a dip in performance, although transformations are often characterized by revenues and earnings that are just failing to grow.

Two critical factors determine the difference between transformations and turnarounds: 1) what is required to execute on the plan, and 2) the amount of runway your current business gives you to do that. More typically turnarounds require significant investments to fix problems. Since turnarounds are happening in a declining revenue or profit environment, companies typically have fewer resources and do not have the luxury of time to accomplish the goal. A transformation of a company whose revenues or profits are merely moving sideways still has good earnings to support investments to effect the transformation, and it has time.

My friend talked to a lot of people, but the one person he didn't speak to was his predecessor. And he didn't ask if it was really a transformation, about why it hadn't broken out before, and what everyone was expecting in terms of resources to get there. He also didn't ask his predecessor about his own experience with "the three envelopes." Had he done so, I think he would have seen the turnaround that the company was in the midst of, and not the transformation everyone wished it was.

Not everyone is willing to be brutally honest—not all outgoing CEOs, not all board members trying to "sell" their company to potential new leadership. Sometimes they are not willing to be honest even with themselves. But if you can get them to talk about two elements of the "three-envelope strategy" during their tenure—about errors of past incumbents and reorganizations—or if you can surreptitiously discover these things on your own, you will be closer to the reality of the company's starting point. You will have a better sense of what has been found to be possible in the past—and what has not been.

You will have an important data point on expenditure rates of past resources and on their effectiveness. This knowledge will validate or invalidate your assessment of the starting place, the destination, and the path to it—all elements of Imperative 3. And in gaining it, you might even get a few chuckles.

Shared Starting Blocks, Shared Finish Lines

Disconnects among the board and management most often originate from mis-shared or miscommunicated views about where the company is starting from or about exactly what kind of company it is. As such, the people, capital, and systems acquisition costs and resource allocation decisions—a few of the most important strategic decisions a company has to make—are often conceived from radically different perspectives. Participating in developing and evaluating company strategy is a key responsibility of boards. Many boards spend considerable time on this activity. But because they didn't ask the right questions—the hard questions—they don't get the right answers. Consensus starting points and finish lines are key to concinnity in corporate governance.

But before you think you've got that covered by settling everything between you and the CEO, think again. You must also consider other stakeholders' views and opinions about your starting point and your destination. The gaps between what stakeholders think about in regard to where you are and where you need to go, and about almost everything else, is the subject of Imperative 4.

A New Framework for Governing

#1 Draw a Line in the Sand

#2 Don't Go Overboard

#3 Assemble at the Same Starting Blocks

#4 Mind the Stakeholder Gap

#5 Manage Your Information Appetite

#6 Be Prepared: Culture and Change Readiness

#7 Don't Leave Compensation to the Experts

#8 Bench Your Inner Coach

#9 Off-Board Well

#10 Cultivate Wisdom

Mind the Stakeholder Gap

Our problem is to bridge the gap, which exists between
where you are now and the goal you intend to reach.
—EARL NIGHTINGALE

I RECENTLY MADE the mistake of going up to our pastor after
church to compliment his sermon. After thanking me, he seized
an opportunity to nab my husband and me for "a little video"
he was working on. My thoughts raced: How did I look? It was
Sunday, after all, so my hair and attire were at least presentable.
Now what?

He wanted us to answer a question while he videotaped
us—no notice, no questions sent via email in advance. On the
spot he wanted us to answer: "Why are you here?"

I was no longer worried about my hair.

So, during the sixty-second walk to the location from
which he wanted to shoot, I ran through my options. A quick
quip certainly could have been in order: "To catch a great sermon . . ." "To listen to awesome music . . ." "Because I feel like
I should be . . ." But I had the feeling he was looking for more,
and my response was for the record, literally. Answering deep

theological questions with no notice is not my forte, but I finally came up with my answer: "To be reminded why I am *here*."

Why Are You Here?

It later occurred to me what a great question this really was, especially for those sitting at the corporate governance table. It also struck me what a good idea it was to ask it without much notice.

What if I asked that question of the CEO? Easy, right? "To grow the bottom line." "Increase sales." "Improve the share price."

All of these are good answers to the question of what the CEO is to *do* here, but what about *why*, and *for whom*? What if I asked the same question of the rest of the board? Would everyone see things the same way?

I once told a friend of mine in the private equity business that sometimes I was amazed that business worked at all. She reminded me that I see a particularly challenged part of the business world. I wondered, *Do I really? Or do I just see what others don't see?* They see real and valid details, but it is very hard for them to see the whole picture. When I was on the inside of a company, I was in the same boat. From a vantage point on the outside, as a trusted advisor, I have a whole different perspective. It is a grave error in corporate governance not to consider the whole picture: every one of the diverse, interconnected stakeholders whose needs and wishes must be juggled within a complex operating environment.

It is the board's job, in partnership with the CEO, to balance company goals with responsibilities. Imagine trying to balance the scales below:

Good Corporate Governance
Balances Goals & Responsibilities

Goals must be achieved in the context of the impact they have on stakeholders. Just as behind every great opportunity there exists potential considerable risk, we must remember that what benefits one stakeholder may impact another less favorably. Stakeholder interests are very interconnected, but usually far from parallel.

For concinnity in corporate governance to exist at all, not only must the interests of the CEO—as a distinct stakeholder compared to the board—be considered, but the interests of many other, often diverse, stakeholders must be considered as well. Not only does harmonious, good governance depend on it, but the board's relationship with the CEO depends on it. In fact, the board's relationship with the CEO depends on careful attention to all stakeholders because, at the end of the day, each and every one of those stakeholders feels that at some level the CEO is accountable to them. And your CEO needs a great relationship with them all.

Do you think average employees don't believe the CEO is

accountable to them? If they do not see executive accountability being lived out in company policy and practice, watch them first lose loyalty, then resist accountability, and then walk. *The Alliance*[17] addresses the urgency of finding alignment between company leadership and talent. True concinnity in corporate governance requires juggling the interests of multiple stakeholders, each of whom has unique expectations. And you and your CEO need healthy boundaries in order to manage all of them. Several of your stakeholders may have assembled at a different starting block from the one where you are perched. All of them think it is *their company.* But who are these diverse stakeholders? Whose company is this, anyway?

Whose Company Is It, Anyway?

I was driving back from an event with the chancellor of a large university early on in my term as CFO of the academic enterprise there. We were speaking about the differences between corporate America, where I had always worked before, and universities. I opined, "The problem you have is that there is no brass ring: at least no singular, shared brass ring. Corporations have a bottom line, if not a stock price, that can serve as a shared corporate brass ring. For the most part, you can get your people focused on that and get them all to pull the rope in the same direction toward that finish line, that goal."

I recall that he took exception to my analysis. I got an earful for the rest of that car ride. He was right. In hindsight, I had oversimplified the variety of corporate stakeholder interests. In reality they look more like this:

....
17   Reid Hoffman et al., *The Alliance: Managing Talent in the Networked Age* (Watertown, MA: Harvard Business Publishing, 2014).

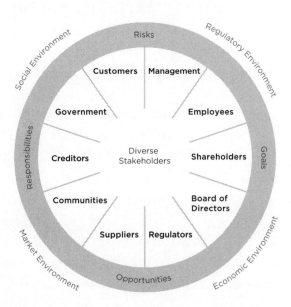

In reality, while many stakeholders appreciate the value of a company's bottom line, there are multiple brass rings in this group, from meteoric stock price increases to cradle-to-grave employment. In rethinking my conversation with the chancellor, I now realize it is possible that my comments sounded like a criticism of the academy. In fact, I was trying to suggest how difficult the chancellor's job really was compared to that of a corporate CEO. To steer a multibillion-dollar enterprise like the one he was leading from point A to point B was a much more complex challenge. The number and diversity of stakeholders he had to contend with makes corporate America seem simple . . . and his stakeholders really saw themselves as shareholders!

Why is this relevant to those of us in business? Because the Academy, if not all large bureaucracies in general, offers helpful case studies in line delineation, competing stakeholder agendas, governance boundaries, and the complexities of a board director's role.

In the case of corporations, ownership is clear: The shareholders own the corporation. They invest their capital in the company in hopes of an attractive return on their investment. But in the case of universities, which don't typically have shareholders per se, the door is open for a variety of stakeholders to claim "ownership" of the entity, much as shareholders do a corporation. If you look at who invests capital in the institution, the most obvious stakeholders, perhaps, are the students and their families. They are hoping for a well-educated, value-adding graduate at the end of the student's tenure. Student and parent priorities may not always align, of course. While I was in college I was particularly interested in my school's investment in a particular bus service that took us into Cambridge on an hourly schedule. Designed for cross-registration between my college and another, my use for it was largely social, but that was what I valued. I am quite sure my parents would have been happy to redirect those resources toward something more likely to add to my post-graduation value on the market.

But another group of stakeholders—and an all-important source of capital for colleges and universities—is the donor base. These are the people—many of them former students—who have accomplished great things in the world and are in the financial position to fund large capital and strategic initiatives for the institution. As any development officer can tell you, these stakeholders often have very specific, very definite objectives in mind for the enterprise and its direction. After all, if you're providing several million dollars as the lead gift for a building fund, you fully expect to say whose name will go on the building.

In the case of employees, one must look at two distinct groups: the faculty and the administration. Forgetting for the moment the flow of academics into administration for varying terms in certain circumstances, faculty have tenure in the technical sense, but often administrators have tenure in terms of years of service. Frequently the administrators, who are the custodians of much of the institutional memory, are those who know "how we do things here." (You could argue that the same is true for the largest of our bureaucracies, the government. I know a guy who has been with state government for almost forty years, a tenure almost unheard of in corporate America these days!) In such cases, who really has more invested in the enterprise?

Within the faculty there are different priorities, as well. I was surprised to learn that the cost, at that time, to recruit a top faculty member who depended on a "wet lab" for his or her pursuit of knowledge was close to a million dollars, while for a mathematician it was the cost of a few pencils and several reams of paper. Likewise the history professor is less excited about spending resources on brick-and-mortar investments than is the biology researcher.

And let's not even get into athletics! You are probably already well aware of the capacity for capital consumption of college sports. But the flipside of that—especially at major universities—is the flood of revenue generated by sports media agreements, ticket sales, and trademark licensing deals.

Still think all of these different stakeholders in the university agree on who owns the place? Hardly.

Students, their parents, donors, faculty, administrators, and athletic directors—all investing time and capital into the organization—each have very different "brass rings." Each stakeholder invests in the university, contributing either time or capital. Each has a valid and vested interest in outcomes, but they are potentially radically different outcomes. Sure, no one actively wants to see another's interests go down the tubes, lest that should reflect badly on their own ability to succeed; but what really ought to occupy management's time, attention, and corporate resources is another thing.

Have the Conversation

Management at all institutions must consider multiple stakeholders, but large bureaucracies like governments and universities face an unparalleled complexity of stakeholders viewing themselves as shareholders. If a board is in place to facilitate the achievement of company goals, companies have an easier time of it, for sure. With that in mind, it is worth studying the university's example and asking the question that university leadership must ask: Exactly what are our company goals? Are they primarily related to the bottom line? Is it growth? Or is it something else?

Sometimes, in companies, we presume it's the bottom line or the stock price. We also presume that the goal is pretty universally shared. But it is well worth the exercise to confirm. You may discover surprising results and opinions generated by a less homogeneous internal shareholder population than you initially thought you were dealing with.

Governance circles are abuzz these days with director challenges from CEOs who develop their own agendas: goals that diverge from what one might more accurately define as corporate goals. There is also a lot of talk about the breathtaking increase in stakeholder diversity and escalating "voice." Having honest conversations is key to avoiding the conflict that prevents concinnity in governance. The board and the CEO must work together in lockstep to identify and segment key stakeholders. They must develop clearly defined roles and responsibilities for executing well-crafted, targeted communication with each of them. No key stakeholders must be left behind to figure out for themselves how the corporation is managing their interests.

Leave No Stakeholder Behind

When I worked in university administration, I had a number of colleagues who had moved from faculty to administration. For sure, there is a different mentality involved when one starts out as an administrator than when one starts out pursuing academics. The same dichotomy exists in healthcare—where you find career administrators working alongside clinicians who have moved into administration—and between new and existing leaders and teams in corporations. There is plenty of room everywhere for culture clash.

One might aptly call the long-timers the long-sufferers. No doubt clinicians who spend their entire careers at one place feel they are required to endure the routine disruptions of new management who, no doubt, will not last long at the organization. In healthcare, the long-term folks include administrators as well as clinicians. Both categories of long-timers must adjust to new leaders, new ideas, new colleagues, and much change.

I have been on both sides of the long-timer/new-guy divide. I have been the one who feels put upon, the one who bristles at the new kid on the block moving too quickly to make changes without really understanding the ecosystem. I have also been the new leader struggling to deal with the recalcitrant long-termers who dig in their collective heels to resist change.

What is a leadership team, including the board and the CEO, to do? Three things:

1. Learn from the past;
2. Respect the past;
3. Leave no stakeholder behind.

The best leaders realize that action must never precede learning. Stephen Covey described it as first seeking to understand, then to be understood.[18] Some leaders implement listening tours or openly give themselves an orientation period in which to learn and not act. Getting the most from any of these techniques depends on suspending criticism and judgment. This is more than just listening actively, as some call it, or empathetically, nodding in understanding. This has more to do with managing your own thoughts as you are going through the learning process.

Very often leaders are in place because they have been hired to make changes, or for the simple reason that their background is different from a predecessor's. Perhaps they were hired to fix something that is broken. When that is the case, it is difficult to listen to how "things are done around here" without reacting

....

18   This is Covey's Habit 5 in *7 Habits of Highly Effective People* (New York: Free Press, 1989).

critically. The mind races to find fault with the status quo. It is our way of bringing logic to why things are the way they are and not the way they could or should be. We are looking to make connections between current process and current results, which may not be everything they could be. These thoughts get in the way of learning useful details and respecting the past. In the process, the long-timers feel disrespected and start down a path of resistance to whatever changes that may come down the pike.

What leaders must do as part of learning from the past is to replace criticism and judgment with a technique I call "compare and contrast." When leaders come across people, processes, or systems that immediately strike them as flawed at best, instead of thinking critically, they should pause. Compare and contrast that person, process, or system with the alternative that you have in mind. *How is this like my way? Unlike my way?* Forcing yourself to identify similarities and differences takes away the one-sidedness of being a critical observer. Finding similarities helps you to find the good in most of what you encounter. Then, you can make sure to keep the good elements in place as you make changes. When you do that, the long-timers will feel heard and respected, and will become more open to change.

Comparing and contrasting what you hear and know is an invaluable exercise when working with your stakeholders. It is not easy, but it is incredibly powerful. I guarantee that you will see things you would have otherwise missed. I further guarantee that you will create less ill will in your own mind as well as in those of others. It is not easy to remember to do this with all stakeholders, but make an effort to take a 360-degree look around yourself and your organization and take account of the diversities. Take your listening and learning tour, armed with your compare-and-contrast technique, to the thought leaders among all of those stakeholders—and you will be far less likely to leave a stakeholder behind.

A final note as you seek to understand before you act: Be up-front about the fact that you are there to learn but that you are also there to find ways to make things better. Acknowledge that you are there to make changes, but insist that with the help and input of your associates, they can be changes of the best sort. Acknowledge that you've been on both sides of changes. Address head-on the equally destructive nature of not understanding change and of being resistant to change.

It's about the Stakeholders, Stupid (All of Them)

Sound bites are often the totality of any news that many Americans get these days, especially when it comes to politics. I remember a tweet I read one morning that said something like, "Obama loses big in Supreme Court decision." No detail about which one, just those thirty-five characters. I won't digress to discuss the pros and cons of that, but this one line is a useful example of how it's about our stakeholders—all of them.

The tweet referred to a decision about employer coverage of employee birth control. My gut reaction upon reading this was not political; I didn't really care about the president that day. I was thinking about other stakeholders whose interests would be impacted by this decision. *I* was thinking about *my* stakeholders, my people: about my employees, my human resource leaders who would have some explaining to do to the confused or worried employees, the women of childbearing age, the husbands whose healthcare expenses would be impacted. Politics is all about the two parties, and the politicians, right? No, it's about many more stakeholders—all of them. It's a valuable lesson to those of us charged with balancing multiple interests.

At the same time this news made the wire, another political story hit the headlines. It too was a reminder about stakeholder management. Howard Baker, a giant in American public service, had passed away. Senator Baker became famous as the "great conciliator" for his record of brokering compromises in the Senate. He is remembered for asking of President Nixon's role in the Watergate scandal, "What did the president know and when did he know it?" He is arguably more remarkable for being, as one legislator described him, "an American first, Tennessean second, and a Republican third,"[19] which speaks to how well Baker juggled the breadth and diversity of his stakeholder base and his own interests.

No doubt the diversity of his stakeholders makes that faced by us corporate types pale in comparison. Nonetheless, we must remember what Senator Baker knew: Owners, shareholders, employees, suppliers, customers, communities, and resources all matter. And we must remember that every decision we make impacts each of them differently. The best leaders realize that and are very deliberate as they navigate choices that will impinge upon one group while benefitting the other. They design their communications around this knowledge. Every time we give raises, for example, it impacts margins and profits, but we know intuitively that it is the right thing to do. Some stakeholder trade-offs are less intuitive, at least at the time the decision is made.

....
19 U.S. Rep. Steve Cohen, D-Tenn. From http://www.timesfreepress.com/news/2014/jun/27/howard-baker-jr-great-conciliator-tennessee-dies/?breakingnews.

A recent experiment made by Facebook offers a good example. The company took a beating for using subscribers in a psychological experiment without their knowledge or consent. The company manipulated the feeds of information to Facebook users and used the responses users posted to measure their reactions to the news. Facebook wanted to learn if its feeds could impact mood, if not behavior. The implications for advertisers were potentially huge if mood and behavior could be manipulated.

In this example, Facebook prioritized the benefits to advertisers, to revenue, and to the bottom line. They did not consider the millions of Facebook users whose emotions were being manipulated. For many it felt like the company was using its customers as lab rats for its own purposes.

The man in charge of the experiment said, "I can understand why some people have concerns about it, and my coauthors and I are very sorry for the way the paper described the research and any anxiety it caused."[20] Personally, I don't consider that an apology. It sounds like the voice of someone who knows he has to say something nice but feels he's done nothing wrong: not sorry for the research, but for the way it was described; not sorry for using customers in a way that takes advantage of them, but for the anxiety some people experienced (read: because they are overly sensitive?). There is an important lesson here, even if the man in charge of the experiment didn't get it: Every decision you make impacts every one of your stakeholders in both positive and negative ways. Great leaders consider the consequences of their decisions at all times. When it is part of your leading

....
20   *Wall Street Journal* online, available at http://online.wsj.com/
articles/furor-erupts-over-facebook-experiment-on-users-1404085840
(accessed November 2, 2014).

and governing methodology, you will make better decisions and leave fewer stakeholders behind.

It is also important to remember that stakeholder engagement is a fragile thing. Good relationships with customers are delicate. Shareholder relations can be a minefield. Not all decisions will be win-win for all stakeholders. The gap between their interests is real and can be wide. Great leaders know this, and they communicate the heck out of their decisions in order to manage expectations. Boards and CEOs must think carefully through their division of labor in this communication process, as boards today are called upon to do more of the communicating than ever before. They must do this hand-in-glove with the CEO.

Interacting with Shareholders Directly

I am sometimes asked when it is appropriate for directors to interact directly with shareholders. You're going to love my answer: It depends. It was considered inappropriate not so long ago; board members rarely interacted directly with shareholders, at least in public companies. But the age of activist investors changed all that. In the largest companies it is becoming more common. But it requires extraordinary skill on the part of the board members who do get involved. The risks of misinformation and triangulation[21] are high, but the legal risks are even higher.

During my tenure managing investor relations for a public company, I received a phone call from one of the buy-side

....

21 In triangulation, one party will not communicate directly with another, but will communicate with a third party. This can lead to the third party becoming part of the "triangle." The concept of triangulation originated in the study of dysfunctional family systems but can describe behaviors in other systems as well, including the corporate boardroom (see http://en.wikipedia.org/wiki/Triangulation_%28psychology%29).

analysts with whom we were in some degree of regular conversation. He phoned after the "window had closed": the period between when companies know what their earnings will be and when they make them public. Once the window has closed, companies are not allowed to talk to the street. As I recall, there was just one more day before we were set to announce our earnings. I was a bit surprised at his call, but nonetheless I asked him what I could do for him.

His reply: "Nancy, what can you tell me?"

My reaction went from surprise to shock to incredulity. I honestly can't remember how I sent him packing, graciously of course, but I can recall all the responses that swirled around in my mind.

"Oh, you want to know what we are reporting tomorrow? Hold on, let me close my door. For you, I'll risk an orange-jumpsuit wardrobe."

Conversations like this really happen. This guy was an owner: not a very ethical one, but a shareholder who was willing to more than push the envelope. In an age of activist investors, it is all about relative value: What can I get that others can't? I expect there is someone reading this who has recently felt pushed up against the envelope by an investor. This area of board activity is not for the faint of heart, nor for the unskilled.

Gap Minding

Communicating the same message requires boards and CEOs to have the same information. Boards today worry that they are not getting the information they need to do their jobs; they started to worry even before taking on the growing mantle of stakeholder communications. How do you get the information you need? Do you just ask anything? Doing this right is Imperative 5 in building a framework for concinnity in governing.

A New Framework for Governing

- **#1** Draw a Line in the Sand
- **#2** Don't Go Overboard
- **#3** Assemble at the Same Starting Blocks
- **#4** Mind the Stakeholder Gap
- **#5** Manage Your Information Appetite
- **#6** Be Prepared: Culture and Change Readiness
- **#7** Don't Leave Compensation to the Experts
- **#8** Bench Your Inner Coach
- **#9** Off-Board Well
- **#10** Cultivate Wisdom

Manage Your Information Appetite

The two words 'information' and 'communication' are often used interchangeably, but they signify quite different things. Information is giving out; communication is getting through. —SYDNEY J. HARRIS

A PRIVATE EQUITY client of mine was debriefing a new portfolio company CEO after their first board meeting. A board member asked the CEO how it went, to which the CEO replied, "I thought the meeting was great. It was just so much work to get ready for!" The board member was both disappointed and amazed. From his perspective, the board had asked the CEO to provide exactly the type of information that they expected he would access every day. From the CEO's perspective, the board was asking for a lot of "extra" information that took a lot of time to pull together.

Once you and your CEO execute Imperatives 1 through 4, determining the information the board needs to help the company achieve its goals and meet obligations to all stakeholders should be pretty straightforward, right? It's not. You and the CEO *must* be on the same page about this.

What's Important to You *and* Your CEO

To repeat a fundamental truth, concinnity in corporate governance depends on a shared view of where you are starting from, where you are going, and how you will get there. At times, when boards and CEOs don't see eye-to-eye on what makes up a good board information packet, what gets presented, or what gets discussed at the board meetings, it may be because they have yet to develop such a shared view.

On other occasions, management may intentionally limit the information that makes its way to the board. It can be management's way of keeping directors' fingers and elbows out of the day-to-day running of the company in order to prevent them from crossing over the governance line into managing operations. While this may suggest a failure to build concinnity around roles, lack of agreement on what information is necessary, what is sufficient, and what is too much can be a symptom of problems in other areas. If you do have differences of opinion about when and how to share information, reflect on why. Differences of opinion on necessary information are among the most common yet least discussed mistakes boards and CEOs make in working together.

Information Asymmetry

Information asymmetry is the imbalance that exists because management always knows more about the company (and potentially the industry) than do the directors. It is considered a risk because a board may not receive information essential to making the kinds of decisions for which it will be held accountable. It can also be a risk due to the possibility that one party takes advantage of another party's lack of information—in this case, management taking advantage of the board or board members taking advantage of others. In the conventional world of corporate governance, where people do not view governing well as coming together in harmony, information becomes a powerful weapon.

> **ASYMMETRIC INFORMATION:** A situation in which one party in a transaction has more or superior information compared to another. . . . Potentially, this could be a harmful situation because one party can take advantage of the other party's lack of knowledge.[22]

I have a good deal of personal experience with information asymmetry. I have been on the inside of companies, a party to determining just what would and would not become part of the information we presented to the board. I have also been an advisor to companies preparing information for their boards and to boards seeking to manage their flow of information. I have pored over a board packet as a director, looking for both the necessary and sufficient information I needed to perform my governance role. Having occupied every seat around the boardroom table helps me to know what should and should not be included in the packet. It has given me a keen sense of when board members are being "managed."

It has also given me the perspective to know that some information asymmetry is the nature of the governance beast; there is no way directors will receive as much information as management. In fact, by definition, directors rely on management to filter information in order to make their jobs possible. So it is critical

. . . .
22   http://www.investopedia.com/terms/a/asymmetricinformation.asp.

to be deliberate about determining what is needed. Getting this right will make everyone's job easier and relationships better.

Information Basics

Your board should have a list of basic information requirements. I find an information distribution matrix to be the most effective tool for that, because it lists necessary information alongside how often and to whom the information should be given.

In the following chart, information items are listed on the left. In the rows across the top you can see the frequency with which the information should be given. Some elements should routinely be included in a board packet; some can be presented as needed or as relevant to a particular meeting. Across the top of the chart you will also see who should receive particular information. Some information, but not all, is appropriate for all board members.

Constructing an information cube ensures a baseline of agreement on information needs. You will want to build your own cube to make sure you have listed the information necessary and sufficient to your particular company and situation. The frequency and distribution will also vary by company.

> It is a very sad thing that nowadays there is so little useless information. —OSCAR WILDE

Good Agendas

You'll notice that "Agenda" is listed at the top of the board information cube. This may not strike you as company information in the context we are using it, but a good agenda sets invaluable parameters on information needs. If you are going to be reviewing management's performance for the year, then you will want to see individual key performance indicators. Having well-thought-out board- and committee-meeting agendas is a great starting point for determining what information, in aggregate, is both necessary and sufficient for the board to do its work. If you begin with a great agenda, you are more likely to come up with a good board packet. If your agenda is insufficient, you and your board colleagues will be asking a lot of questions. If you include too much unnecessary information, you may find it difficult to get through the agenda or the information in the time allowed.

ITEM	FREQUENCY		RECIPIENT	
	Routine	Periodic	Full Board	Committees
Agenda	X		X	X
Dashboards	X		X	X
Strategic Plan		X	X	X
Risk Management Plan (ERM)		X	X	
Executive Comp Plan		X		X
Succession Plan		X		X
Annual Goals		X	X	X
Company Metrics and KPIs	X		X	X
Company Financials (Audit, Budget, and Plan)	X		X	X

Management teams seeking to keep certain information out of the hands of board members can accomplish that by just leaving important stuff out. Or they can try to bury you with unnecessary information. As a board member, you should be alert to both tactics. Getting a solid agenda is a key starting point. Ask yourself if the material provided sticks to the agenda and gives you what you need to discharge your responsibilities to help the company get where it is going, consider risks adequately, and juggle stakeholder interests. It is important not to be slavish to the same agenda for every meeting, especially over time; business environments are incredibly dynamic, and what is necessary and sufficient today can be neither tomorrow. Just as in the setting of lines between boards and management, we need to realize that "normal" information flow today may not work tomorrow. In the ongoing efforts to balance information necessity and sufficiency, board members must be open to a new normal. Flexibility is vital.

Good Metrics

The second item listed in the sample board information cube is an information dashboard. A company dashboard is the equivalent of the instrument panel in a car; everything that you need to know to drive is centralized for easy viewing. While there are some pretty sophisticated dashboard software programs, including some that are integrated into a company's management information or enterprise management system, a reasonably effective and powerful dashboard can be created with a simple spreadsheet. The critical piece is to determine the key metrics of performance and to measure and review them regularly.

Knowing the company's mission and goals and understanding how they are measured constitute table stakes for that portion of your governance role. You need to be able to see and evaluate the progress of the company and its leadership team toward and against these goals. Performance should be presented to you in both a longitudinal (over time) and latitudinal (compared to competitors/peers, fashion, etc.) format. The board and the CEO must agree on what metrics will be used to measure the company's progress. The metrics should consider achievements on the path toward your goals, how you will reach the company's goals, and what resources will be required and when.

Reviewing its own performance is a very important role for the board. A board committed to reviewing its own work is a powerful statement to the CEO: "Yes, we are reviewing you, but we are also reviewing ourselves." There are a number of consulting firms that can help with this, or there are associations, such as the National Association of Corporate Directors (NACD), that provide tools to help a board evaluate itself. Whether engaging a consultant or doing it yourself, it is important to agree upon a process and frequency for evaluating the board. As with measuring company progress, metrics are appropriate for board evaluations. If the board has a dashboard for its own work, this can simplify the evaluation process. If you have good metrics, board information can be greatly simplified, and all that is required is for management to give color on those results metrics, either in summary form or verbally, at the board meetings.

Good Timing

We've established that developing and evaluating company strategy is one of the board's most important jobs, but when is it appropriate to address it with the board? For all of its activities, and the information related to them, the board must build consensus on the frequency at which it reviews strategy. Development of strategy is often an annual topic of discussion at either a board meeting or a board retreat. And, if the company is operating in a very dynamic and rapidly changing environment, from a competitive standpoint (or characterized by other dynamic disrupters), it may be appropriate for the board to revise company strategy on a more regular basis.

There are other directorial duties that the board will typically address on a more periodic basis. These often include an annual review of management performance, and a review of the board's performance, which may be annual or every couple of years. In addition to assessing board (and CEO) performance, there are other board matters that are appropriate for periodic review. Depending on the stage and size of the company, and also the rate of change it is experiencing (including rate of growth), review and oversight of company policies may occur annually or every few years.

Appropriate Distribution

Another aspect of board information to consider is whether or not the information is for the consumption of the full board or for committees of the board. Just as directors rely on management to filter information, board members look to committees to do the same thing. A member of the audit committee is going to take a deeper dive into the financials than a member of the compensation committee. Likewise, the compensation committee will review more detailed executive performance data than might an audit committee member. Separation of duties through the committee structure allows for optimal management of the depth and breadth of information shared for communication and digestion.

Agreeing on the basic information, getting it to the right people at the right time, and being deliberate about revisiting and communicating are game changers. Board meetings become far more effective and fun, because relationships improve when everyone is appropriately informed. The board members have then only to ask the *right questions*, not every question that comes to their minds.

What to Ask

I have a cousin who is a kindergarten teacher; she has the best stories. One of my favorites is about how she manages all the whining in her classroom. Let's face it, when you're five, it's your job to whine. Most whining is a product of learning how to share; somebody else has what you want, but when you're five, you think it is something you can't live without. One of my cousin's jobs is to teach her kids the difference.

Her trick? Every single time one of her kids tells her they *need* something, she asks, "Do you need it? Or do you *want* it?" It is a terrific question for those of us seated around the boardroom table to ask ourselves with regard to information. The questioning board member is an invaluable asset to the company. But being the right kind of questioning board member requires discipline, as well as insight.

I can relate to feeling the urge to ask company leadership teams just about anything that comes to mind, so it was very gratifying when a fellow board member described me recently as "the one who asks all the right questions." This is the ultimate compliment for a board member. If you ask every question that comes to mind, there will never be enough time to get the critical questions answered. An unmanaged barrage of questions can keep board meetings from being practical in length, which may indicate a lack of structure around the meetings themselves. It can also indicate that directors are not curbing their appetite for information; they are asking for data that they want, not information that they need. The harm in asking every question that comes to mind is: 1) it can lead to more work for company leadership, straining resources, and 2) it can keep the board from being able to address other, often more critical, issues.

Whom to Ask

So who should answer all of your questions, once you have figured out which ones to ask? Does it go without saying that board inquiries should begin, but not end, with the CEO? I was speaking with a new CFO whose audit committee chair had reached out to her for a getting-to-know-you lunch. The CFO welcomed the opportunity to start off her working relationship with her key new board interface person on a positive, informal note. She thought, as I don't doubt the audit committee chair did, that the first board meeting was probably not the best place to launch their working relationship.

The CFO appropriately let the CEO know that the audit chair had made the overture and that she had accepted it. But, the CEO made it clear that he was not interested in the CFO meeting with the audit chair without him.

Seriously?

Bad start for the new CFO? Maybe. Red flag for the board audit committee chair? Quite possibly.

In this case I would imagine that the audit chair felt that it was quite appropriate for him to meet one-on-one with the CFO of the company—which it should have been—but he did not think to advise the CEO in advance. It is possible that the CEO could have been made to see the situation the same way, had he been in the loop from the beginning or advised in advance.

I had a partner who believed that the worst mistake made by the board of a company he had worked for, as a CFO, was not getting the answers to the hard questions from the right sources. They did not always ask the hard questions, and they were usually content to have the answers served up by the CEO himself. Sometimes the CEO actually directed the board's questions to a junior-level person in the finance organization, bypassing the CFO altogether. As a result, the board members received either prepackaged answers or too-detailed information from the wrong people.

The way CFOs and CEOs complement, balance, and challenge each other is altogether different from the relationship between the CEO and those outside the C-suite. The right answers don't always live at 30,000 feet *or* at ground level. Oftentimes other members of the C-suite have a level of detail, self-questioning, and experience with the subject matter that the CEO does not have. But those in the lower levels of the organization often don't have the perspective needed to present a balanced or accurate picture, even as they have more detailed knowledge or experience than the CEO. In the case of my partner's company, the board missed important information about the resources needed for a major change in product line strategy. Had they had that information, considerable losses could have been prevented.

So it is critical that the board not only ask the hard questions, but ask them of the right people and do so with full respect for the governance-leadership line. The board must have an agreed-upon way of working with other leaders in the C-suite in order to maintain good working relations with the CEO. Just as the CEO must know when to "zoom in and zoom out,"[23] board members must know when they need to reach closer to the source to get their questions answered. But they must do so with permission from the CEO. If they believe the CEO unreasonably limits access, then it is time for the board as a whole to revisit the topic, first in executive session, then with the CEO.

I must confess intimate familiarity with actively controlling what information boards were allowed, and not allowed, to have . . . and it was not always motivated by the best of intentions. Sometimes it was an issue, plain and simple, of control: of information or of access to different people who may provide different information than the CEO wants revealed. This kind of intentional control of information flow creates ineffectual board members, frustration, and ill will. It is why boards increasingly fear the risks of information asymmetry.

Boards must be ever aware of their need to overcome the information imbalance and get what they need in order to provide effective oversight and advice. They need to improve the quality and usefulness of the information they receive about the business and also about the industry. They must consider if and when to seek information from independent sources,

....
23   Rosabeth Moss Kanter, "Managing Yourself: Zoom In, Zoom Out," *Harvard Business Review* online, available at http://hbr.org/2011/03/managing-yourself-zoom-in-zoom-out/ar/1 (accessed November 2, 2014).

which can be useful to both management and the company if they are well informed. But whom do you ask? When should you approach sources outside the company?

The short answer? Almost never. But read that as *almost* never, not *never*. Obviously directors are privy to substantial confidential information that should not be shared outside of the company. They must also realize that whenever they are speaking outside of the company, like it or not, people will presume that at some level the information and opinions they have are windows into the company. So great care must be taken. But board members are often appointed for their industry expertise—usually for their functional expertise—and always for their intellect and ability to question and evaluate. This is how they contribute to the company's goals. This is how they respect and do their best to preserve the interests of all stakeholders. So, the roles they play, the people they know, and the worlds in which they live outside of the company expose them to information that could be very valuable to the enterprise. This information provides much-needed perspective that company insiders are rarely privy to and may provide answers to questions that are either not available inside the company or that appropriately challenge what the board member is hearing inside the company and at board meetings. CEOs want intel that board members can bring to the table from their other lives.

But board members must be mindful that there is a right and a wrong way to gather relevant information outside the company. For one, the gathering of information from people and organizations related to the company, related entities, outside service providers, peers, or competitors should almost always be done with the CEO in the loop. Gathering of information from unrelated outside sources should be done in general and indirect ways so as not to reveal confidential information or strategy. Remember, people will always be looking to divine company strategy or more from you. This is especially true for public companies, but is not limited to them.

When to Invite Management

A related discussion directors should have is when it is appropriate for members of senior management to attend board meetings. This can be an excellent topic to discuss in executive session, without management present—at least at first. If you sit on a board where management never attends board meetings and directors do not have relationships with leadership beyond the CEO, there may be cause for concern. Likewise, if there exists no protocol for when and how to work with members of the C-suite, it is likely that conditions are ripe for miscommunication and misunderstanding, if not overt conflict. This is a topic that must be addressed head-on by the board in concert with the CEO.

When to Revisit

Most likely your board has a history of various information flows, both to the board as a whole and to specific committees. Oftentimes, new board members are reluctant to ask too many questions. Certainly while your appointment is new, it is a good time to focus on being a good listener. Having said that, a fresh pair of eyes can see things that more tenured board members do not see, so the questions new members ask can be invaluable.

I was appointed to a board finance committee, the primary

role of which was overseeing the investment of assets. The committee consisted of very senior, nationally respected investment professionals. The work of the committee was governed by a charter, and there was an investment policy that provided guidance to both the committee and to outside investment advisors. The fact that there was such depth of expertise on the committee bought me time to get up to speed. This isn't always the case for new board or committee members, so I took advantage of the opportunity. Despite my own qualifications as a finance expert, I had a lot to learn about the history and program of this committee, its advisors, and the funds we oversaw. This committee had a great deal of information to review for each of its meetings, so I spent my first few meetings consuming volumes of data (evoking memories of my early tenure on that credit committee that reviewed Bradlees). Over time I began to realize that there were governing documents that were not a part of our regular review. Company management was more than happy to share that information, and once I had it I realized that it had not been reviewed in quite a long time. In fact, in some important ways and for some very good reasons, we were operating outside of policies established several years earlier.

The committee was doing a good job, and fund performance was acceptable. But at some point the committee needed to revisit its own governance documents. Because I was a process person, that exercise was not unwelcome to me; it was just going to take a fair bit of time. It is important to realize that not all of your colleagues will be process-oriented, so don't expect everyone to cheer if you find yourself in my situation. But done right, good governance rules and process documentation can make your job easier and more fun. It allows you to avoid conflict both with your board colleagues and with your CEO and her leadership team. The documentation will go a long way to orienting and integrating new board and committee members, which is a process about which boards can hardly be too deliberate.

Board Orientation

It is not rocket science, but asking the right—and just the right—questions is impossible without good board orientation. You would be surprised at how often this crucial element of board effectiveness is overlooked. Many boards rely on management, and that is fine, but the responsibility for orientation lies with the board. So have a protocol for your board's orientation practices, and follow it. Have a checklist, a standard package of basic information, and detailed, relevant data for committee assignments, and keep them up to date.

Tours are a great tool for acclimating new board members and introducing them to the appropriate players on the inside of the company. Some boards assign "board buddies" to assist in individual new-member orientation. Board buddies can be very effective, as long as the buddies are educated on what it is they are to do. I had a delightful board buddy once—delightful, but not particularly helpful. The way in which new board members are introduced to your company and to their specific roles and responsibilities is a cornerstone in the foundation of concinnity in corporate governance.

Some companies are committed to continuing education for their boards. With the rate of change of the environments—business, social, regulatory, and economic— in which boards must do their work, continuing education is a great tool. There are consulting firms and associations, like the National Association of Corporate Directors (NACD), that can provide educational resources. A friend of mine attended an NACD national conference with his entire board. Learning can be a powerful tool for improving board effectiveness and working relations with the CEO and her team. Learning at the same time is even more powerful and can jumpstart a board's progress toward concinnity in corporate governance . . . as long as you are mindful that, even now, much of what is being taught about corporate governance still sees the boardroom as the old-school "us vs. them" view. Good education for the new board member *and* the seated board member is critical to ensuring appropriate information flow.

The Complexity of Financial Information

You will want to be especially clear on the necessary and sufficient information to share in regard to financials, as this area presents unlimited opportunity for misinformation and information overload. You most assuredly will be reviewing, if not approving, your company's financial plans, and it is worth discussing the existence of multiple plans and how they affect your role as a director.

My personal philosophy, developed when I was working in the public company arena, is that one financial plan is not enough. I know . . . I can hear half of you saying, "What?" But, hear me out. This is not about reducing transparency in the interest of creating cushions—something an old banking client of mine did through the use of what he called his "side buckets," or that an old colleague did using accounts only he controlled. It is about giving people the appropriate financial information they need to do their jobs. So, hear me out.

In the context of publicly reporting companies, there is a price to pay for being public: meeting the street's earnings expectations. When I ran my company's interactions with Wall Street investors, companies that did not provide earnings "guidance" to help the analysts develop their own earnings estimates were rare birds. But now more companies are declining to provide such guidance for some very valid reasons. I can argue both sides of the case. Let's presume your company is public and you do provide earnings guidance. Once provided, your investors and the sell-side investment banking analysts who cover your company expect you to deliver on those numbers. Can you blame them? We could debate whether or not markets should punish companies that miss earnings estimates (often for unforeseeable and justifiable reasons) with large sell-offs that produce marked drops in share price. But that is a real risk. So what kind of financial forecasting are you going to do as the basis for guiding them— your stretch goal? Hardly.

More likely, your CFO will take a conservative approach. I used to call it my "chip-shot plan." It was my way of ensuring that we did not miss the street's expectations—if I had anything to do with it—in the event that anything impacting earnings was within our control. Remember, what you are doing is *appropriately* managing the information flows to stakeholders.

So let's say your company has a chip-shot plan it uses to guide the street. Do you really think that is the plan to use in holding management—let's say at the division or operating

level—accountable? Not on your life. You want the operational leadership stretching to achieve the goals that will
impact their own performance. The probability of a miss in
one corner of the company is high, especially if you run anything like a global enterprise. So you want the operating plan
to challenge line management, but the street plan to contain
a margin for error. Without it, the plan used to manage the
street has a higher probability of error than you can tolerate.

So now we're up to two financial plans: the chip-shot plan
for the street and the "stretch goal" plan for internal use. Should
there be more? Well, let me just say that from the insider's view,
your role as board member is just a notch or so below that of
the outside investors and analysts. As a board member, you are
now in the category of someone the company does not want
to disappoint. I have been at companies that had one plan on
which to manage insiders, one plan for the board, and a third
plan for the street. I have also been at companies that had only
two. Having multiple plans is an effective way to manage a company. As a board member you must appreciate this and work
with your CEO and her leadership to manage for success inside
and outside the company.

Family-owned and privately owned companies don't have
Wall Street to manage, but they often have outside debt holders
who could be categorized as investors. If shareholders don't like
surprises, how do you think lenders feel about them? Multi-
budget scenarios have relevance in these situations, too.

At the end of the day, or in each of these cases, *appropriate*
financial information is what creating multiple financial plans
is about: making sure various stakeholders have what they need
to lead and govern well together.

Satisfying Everyone's Information Appetite

The good news is that governing through Corporate Concinnity sets the stage for managing the information dissemination process as a team, as opposed to being adversaries. This is especially true in the emerging role of board members in dealing directly with shareholders.

Remember, lack of concurrence about what information the board needs to do its job can be the symptom of serious problems that will preclude creating concinnity in governing. Disagreements around this fundamental element of governing can also create problems. Working through it provides a marvelous opportunity for the board and the CEO to lead and govern in harmony, creating a foundation for frank, honest, and complete communication. This collaborative effort can be especially powerful when developing a working relationship with a *new* CEO. In fact, the relationship between a new CEO and the board is of such importance that managing it well is its own imperative, or at least the beginning of Imperative 6. The board has a unique role in creating conditions that will enable a new CEO to create Corporate Concinnity in leading, something the board truly needs her to do. It is all about culture and change readiness.

A New Framework for Governing

#1 Draw a Line in the Sand

#2 Don't Go Overboard

#3 Assemble at the Same Starting Blocks

#4 Mind the Stakeholder Gap

#5 Manage Your Information Appetite

#6 Be Prepared: Culture and Change Readiness

#7 Don't Leave Compensation to the Experts

#8 Bench Your Inner Coach

#9 Off-Board Well

#10 Cultivate Wisdom

Be Prepared: Culture and Change Readiness

Culture eats strategy for breakfast.

—PETER DRUCKER

INDIVIDUAL PERFORMANCE IS the foundation of corporate performance. A great CEO has remarkable power to drive company excellence. But cultural roadblocks can stall even stellar individual performance to the point of impotence. In my human capital consulting days, we used to say that the world's greatest new CEO is powerless to drive company performance when faced with leading an organization that is ill prepared for what he or she could bring to the table. A lack of organizational readiness for constructive change is a huge barrier to progress, and also to achieving Corporate Concinnity in the boardroom.

ORGANIZATIONAL READINESS: The condition of being prepared, culturally and structurally, for significant change; having in place the foundations for accepting and participating in constructive transitions.

Unless your organization has gone through a great deal of assessment it is unlikely that your board has a good handle on organizational change readiness. It doesn't just happen, especially in times of rapid change, and *especially* in times of change in the C-suite. I have seen a shocking number of exceptional leaders run aground in organizations that were collectively unreceptive to the change they attempted to bring or, worse, were hostile to it and to them. This can be a real risk in very large, bureaucratic organizations, especially those where the human capital at the top changes with more frequency than middle-level management. The board must have a very good sense of organizational readiness at the C-suite level, if not at the middle level as well. Organizational readiness has to do with culture, morale, corporate values, and personal ethics as they play out in the workplace.

In a post-mutual-loyalty (corporate-employee) age, companies often lack the trust and respect needed to create constructive working relationships and healthy corporate cultures. In fact, many of my clients are organizations going through considerable change. They are grappling with the structural and cultural aspects of navigating these transitions and the governance and leadership elements that drive them. I've seen rock star execs fail when companies were neither organizationally nor emotionally ready to receive or participate in creating constructive change. This is not only something boards can lead on; it is their responsibility to do so.

There is much talk about the importance of the "tone" at the top and its centrality to healthy organizational culture. Most people think "at the top" refers to the CEO, but they should also think "board." As a director, do you have a firm handle on the tone in your company? The mood in the C-suite? Morale in middle management? The board is the ultimate tone setter. How has yours impacted tone throughout the organization? If you are not certain of it, now is a good time to *stop* and consider it. Times of change in leadership in general, and of the CEO in particular, are important times to reevaluate. Even if you think you are about to bring in the greatest CEO in the history of the C-suite, you must examine your organization's readiness for its new leader. The board needs to do everything in its power to ensure the success of an incoming CEO. The price of not doing so is astronomical. Research estimates the net cost of CEO failures at eighteen months on the job to be twenty to thirty times annual cash compensation.[24] Furthermore, research shows that new CEO failure rate is 34.9 percent and 18.5 percent for outsider and insider CEOs respectively.[25] Failures in the areas of culture and change readiness are a large contributor to these failures. Boards must address these obstacles. There are several varieties and flavors.

NIH (Not Invented Here)

Let me dig a little deeper into what I mean by the cultural and structural aspects of organizational readiness for change. One of the most common roadblocks to change is the well-known NIH (not invented here), which is also articulated as, "We don't do it that way." I had a client company whose new investors hired me to help evaluate leadership. The investors in this

....

24   See http://chiefexecutive.net/the-costs-of-ceo-failure.

25   Booze & Co. CEO Succession Report, http://www.strategyand.pwc.com/media/uploads/Strategyand_CEO-Succession-Study-2011_Extended-Study-Report.pdf.

situation prided themselves on their ability to invest in great management teams, but had become concerned that one member of their C-suite might not be the right player. I have yet to meet an investor group that doesn't consider investing in great management teams a core competency. But, as is often the case, the management team does not always fulfill expectations as time goes on, which was the case here.

Over the course of trying to work with the company, I began to have difficulty communicating with them. The company executive who had picked up the ball to work with me—let's call her Dorothy—was not only difficult to reach, she communicated different fact sets than the private equity firm: different needs, different timetables. Inasmuch as all of the players were only a few weeks into this new relationship, the confusion was not wholly unexpected. But just how much of a problem they had had become clear to me in just one phone call.

It went something like this:

> Me: I understand you are the point person to set up a meeting with the senior team to debrief on our last conference call.

> Dorothy: That won't really be necessary. I can tell you what you need. But, honestly, there is nothing we can tell you now. We just need more candidates from you.

> Me: Well, let me explain to you why I think this meeting will help me help you.

Dorothy: Here's what I know now . . . and we'll just have to get back to you in a couple of weeks. But send us more candidates.

Me: I understand where you are coming from, but Mr. Brown at the PE firm suggested that he wanted this meeting.

Dorothy: Well, that's because he doesn't know yet how we do things here.

Wow. He doesn't know how we do things here? All I could think was, *Dorothy, you are not in Kansas anymore. You just don't know it yet.*

"We don't do it that way" is a powerful organizational roadblock. In this case it delayed making a key leadership appointment for months. This, in turn, delayed progress on achieving the goals both the investors and management had for the company. Often the chain of events triggered by changes in new ownership—new people, new processes, new systems—creates structural obstacles for all of the players. But when cultural barriers pop up, such as NIH or "we don't do it that way," they can be even more disruptive to progress.

Expectation Asymmetry

Another cultural barrier that is equally destructive is expectation asymmetry, which occurs when different players—boards, CEOs, other leaders—don't share the same view of the end game.

I once heard a client say, "Our owners could flush their entire investment in our company, and they could still have a really great year in terms of their fund returns." He was like a cold stone statue when he said it, as if by being frozen he would be immune to the devastation of such a reality. *Wow,* I thought, *that was one of the more frank yet discouraging comments I ever heard from a client. Talk about a defeatist attitude!*

What he really communicated to me in his statement was that he didn't feel as if his actions mattered. It also communicated a disconnect between what the board thought and what management thought about the company's position and end game. In other words, I was quite sure that the board was extremely invested in the success of the company, this executive's fatalistic attitude notwithstanding. They were suffering from expectation asymmetry.

I expect that the reality was that the board members, all fund guys, had done well on another investment. Good for them. But did that really mean that they did not care about the return on investment in my client? I think not. I think they cared a great deal about this particular company. However, I expect that their outsized returns on some other company were talked about more than the goals for my client. Private equity funds depend on outsized returns on a small percentage of their investments to balance out the poor returns and losses on other investments. Unfortunately, this particular member of the management team thought it didn't matter to the investors how his company performed. This is a perfect example of expectation asymmetry, a rather common and potentially devastating disconnect between management teams and their boards/owners. Communication around expectations—a lot of it—between these players is the best defense against expectation asymmetry.

Change Resistance Awareness

Soon after herniating a disk in my neck, I learned that healing would take a whole lot longer than I expected (or wanted). I was handed big change, and I didn't want it. I had to deal with my resistance, and tap into new sources of patience and positive energy.

Organizational change is much the same, especially when it occurs at senior levels. Just as I had to engage in a process of becoming pain-free and building back up to "normal" efficiency and activity levels, businesses must learn to work *with* limits to change readiness, not *around* them. I call this "change-resistance awareness." Boards must develop good radar, patience, and techniques to turn negative barriers into positives.

One Sunday afternoon, despite being banned from playing golf while recovering, I joined my husband on the course to ride in the cart and enjoy the day. I sneaked in a putter, promising I would use it only if there was no pain or numbness in my neck or arm before and after. So my husband turned it into a little game. I would putt from wherever he chipped onto the green. We kept score, and tied on all but one hole. My spirits jumped about a thousand feet that day. I wasn't the helpless, worthless blob I felt I was growing into! It was amazing how a little bit— and I mean *little* bit—of positivity can go such a long way in a sea of negatives.

The same is true in the workplace. Think about how much workforce fear and unhappiness cropped up during the last recession. Think about the mood in your own company, even now. Odds are that even without a public proxy battle, a CEO-shareholder struggle, or plummeting share prices, there are still pockets of your organization where things aren't always coming up roses. If change resistance is causing pain in your company, you must make a conscious effort to boost morale. Granted, your involvement with most individuals in the company is indirect, but you have both the power and the responsibility to impact morale for the good. Within a positive and constructive culture, people are motivated to work together for productive change, which is in turn essential to Corporate Concinnity. What little positive pebble can you, as a leader, drop into that sea?

One evening I went to a retirement party for a physician who had been in a small practice for the bulk of his career. There were staff members at the event who had worked for him for twenty or more years. As someone who has recruited and placed dozens of executives through the years, I know these tenures are way off the bell curve. There were professional associates there who said they felt more like family than coworkers. The room was overflowing with positive morale from people who felt as if they and their work mattered. They stuck around way longer than the average worker as a result, and the practice was enormously successful. It's a message larger organizations should heed. How can they engender feelings such as these workers had?

> Culture is one thing and varnish is another.
> **—RALPH WALDO EMERSON**

Larger organizations can take another important lesson in change management from that night, one that is not just for the healthcare sector. While the retiree and his staff were enjoying a slide show of great moments over the years, I overheard a number of physicians sharing horror stories in the back room. Most centered around how healthcare administrators don't care about physicians anymore—don't even like them! One healthcare administrator they mentioned had been a practicing physician in his previous role, but they viewed him as someone who purposefully avoided doctors. Big ouch!

Healthcare, in fact, could be the poster child for the pitfalls of change management, because it is arguably a sector most in turmoil from a leadership and governance standpoint. This is partly because the fundamental business models have been turned upside down. In concert with that, brand new alliances are being formed and old ones are being disrupted. All the players engaged in working together to lead and govern healthcare organizations are looking across new tables at new people. Without a conscious effort to create conditions for concinnity, battle lines can and will be drawn.

In the previous chapter we talked about the fragility of stakeholder engagement. In healthcare there is much talk of patient engagement, which is seen as a critical element in moving the needle on healthcare costs in America. I couldn't agree more with this view, but there is another stakeholder group whose engagement is being eroded. In many healthcare organizations, efforts to address costs are leaving physician engagement behind. Negative morale is reaching a very destructive level at some of these companies. Remember, it's about *all* stakeholders. Of course, not all can benefit equally, so communication is essential.

Having a leader like the administrator mentioned in the preceding anecdote—one who avoids a disenfranchised group—is very bad. The cost of this hit to morale will eventually be quite high. You think patient engagement is hard? Just wait until the caregivers go snarky. Leaders in healthcare must redouble their efforts to drop a little positivity into the pool as they address morale issues that result from change and from being ill prepared for change. But if you are not in healthcare, you have your own stakeholders whose engagement is being eroded. Who are they? What are you doing to convert this negative energy?

Mind you, it doesn't take much: just a few key wins. What is important to your constituency? Keep asking yourself that question until you have a list of things you *can* offer them in addition to those you can't. How important was it, in the scheme of things, that I matched my husband in putting? What I really wanted was to whack my Big Bertha driver 200 yards, but I would have to wait another couple of months for that. In the meantime, I planned to work on my putting, maybe even my short game, with a little pitching and chipping action around the greens. When I thought about it, my short game needed work anyway. It was a place I could work constructively and nourish myself emotionally. Similarly, the gift of being intentional and deliberate when addressing negativity in your workforce and in your leadership is a gift that will keep on giving.

We Are Not Broken

In today's world, CEO changes are made because someone is unhappy: Either performance has suffered and the company, as a whole, is unhappy, or the CEO finds an opportunity (or it finds her) that appears to offer more happiness. The board should look closely at the reasons for the departure (see the envelope stories in Imperative 3). Rarely is it just the fault of a single actor, regardless of the power of a rock star CEO. There are always organizational contributors to lack of success. Understanding them before hiring a new person will ensure you hire into the strength needed to deal with them.

I worked with an organization that was losing its CEO to retirement. His tenure had been very long, and he was beloved by most of the organization. They knew the risk of hiring a clone of him, or an anti-him, so they hired an interim. They made very clear to the interim CEO that the company was not broken; it "just needed new leadership." These four words can spell cultural or structural barriers to change that will erode your chances to develop concinnity.

It was not until a couple of years into the permanent successor's term that the organization began to realize that there were some ways in which the company was very much broken. It was unfortunate. Valuable time was lost that could have been devoted to progress. Even a healthy organization has broken elements. Don't wait for the new CEO to find them. In fact, finding them before you hire will ensure you hire someone capable of addressing them. Interims can do that for you if you and they are intentional about it.

Interim Power

In most cases, a period of interim leadership can facilitate organizational readiness for change. It is an incredibly powerful resource in the board's toolkit when well structured. Organizations routinely appoint the closest warm body to be interim, one inside the company. These folks have great institutional knowledge and can keep current projects on track, but they are not especially well positioned to evaluate organizational readiness for change.

Some organizations understand the value of bringing in an outsider, but look for the lowest-cost provider of interim leaders. Expensive mistake. Serving well as an interim is a unique skill in its own right. It takes a special skill set to move into an organization, know where to go to "find the buried bodies," as one of my partners used to describe it, and work independently as needed (much as an insider can) to evaluate the situation. And if the interim has no interest in the permanent position, all the better. With no dog in the fight, interims can be more objective in their evaluations.

I worked with an organization that hired a seasoned CEO with no previous interim experience. The organization required him to get interim training before he started, which caused him to chafe more than a little. In hindsight, however, I think he saw the wisdom of it. Someone who has deep interim experience knows how to play the different, tricky role that comes without the presumed authority and acceptance that permanent appointees enjoy. I cannot stress enough the value of previous experience in hiring an interim.

Equally important is the assessment of organizational readiness, which a great interim can do well. In all cases, assessing organizational readiness increases the probability of identifying organizational roadblocks to new leadership and cultural problems that can derail change at the top. Ensuring that your company is ready for the greatest CEO since sliced bread is an important responsibility of the board.

Organizational readiness should be of paramount importance to your board to ensure the success of the rock star CEO you are going to hire.

Personnel Is Personal

I recall a case study on the topic of talent management from my MBA coursework. The company in the study was expanding overseas and needed to determine which exec to send over to run the new operation. In the case, which was led by a very knowledgeable and impressive executive from a large New York company, two candidates were presented. From a credentials perspective, one candidate—we'll call her Ruth—was more qualified to execute on the initiatives needed to make the expansion work. The other candidate—we'll call him Jack—was quite capable in his own right. Moreover, Jack had no personal issues that would have required significant workarounds in order for him to take an overseas assignment. Ruth, on the other hand, had an older in-law living with her, and it appeared from all of the data in the case that dealing with her in-law would have presented tremendous, if not insurmountable, difficulties. Who would you have chosen?

I think just about everyone in the class chose Jack. It just seemed a sure bet. Some might not have wanted to put Ruth through all that difficulty, but for the most part the class analyzed Ruth's personal situation as a deal breaker. The assumption was that while she was great, she was not a transferrable executive, or if she did transfer, it wouldn't work for the long term due to her personal situation. Turnover, in the short term, of course, would produce disruptive change for the company to address.

The "right answer," according to the professor, was to offer the position to Ruth. There is no way you, as a manager, can know all of the facts of someone's personal situation, and you must make a decision based on qualifications. You never know what things people are able and willing to change unless you give them a chance; talk to them about it. Choosing Jack meant making a decision based on considerable assumptions rather than choosing the best talent.

In the real case, in fact, the company chose Ruth. She took the assignment, put her mother-in-law in a nursing home—something she and her husband had been considering for some time—and had a successful long-term overseas engagement. Ruth was ready for change; we all presumed she was not. It was a dangerous presumption.

It is important to remember—important enough to repeat—that you *never* know all of the facts of the personal situation or which way it will go. It is also important to remember that readiness for change is everyone's job, even to the point of dealing with change caused by personal situations you don't know about. You never know how personal change will play out.

I spoke recently with a former client who confided that she was facing increasing family pressure to make changes in her work situation. Even though she was in a position to benefit substantially from a robust, long-term incentive plan, she was considering giving it all up in order to make things work better on the home front. I never would have expected that from her, and neither did her company. The company was unprepared when she resigned; they thought there was no way the exec would make the change, given the financial incentives they had put in place. They weren't thinking about the change trump card: the personal situation.

I would modify the message from my B-school class all those years ago as follows: Always choose the absolute best candidate, based on business facts such as experience, expertise, and capabilities. Leave the unknown, assumed intangibles, and personal facts, to the individual. But as a leader, *always* be aware of the intangibles, known and unknown. As board members we must always think about change when it comes to the C-suite. Change will happen there sooner than you think, probably for reasons you are not predicting.

Much of this chapter has been about preparing your organization for change, an important piece of the framework for concinnity in governance. But good governance is unsustainable unless the players in the governance game—the board, the CEO, and the C-suite—plan for changes within the team itself. When you make leadership decisions based on skills and competencies, you can be sure you've made the right choice. If you take the next step and plan for change not to happen as and when you expect with your team, you will be ready for it. In the process, you can engender a culture that embraces change, as opposed to fighting it.

The Chef Knob

Remember Dorothy, my client's employee who was not in Kansas anymore but did not know it? She was in for some kind of big changes. Your company must be prepared for change. The board has a big role to play in that, as it does in establishing the best culture. But it is not your job to control the pace of that change. When my late husband was in graduate school, he and a post-doc were conducting a complicated physics experiment in their lab at Yale. Not only were my PhD-seeking spouse and his colleague committed to the pursuit of new knowledge in science, they were also committed to having a good time and maintaining their sense of humor through the drudgery their research often entailed. The problem was that getting hydrogen atoms to behave the way you want and on demand is not always an easy task. Their experiment involved sending the atoms down a tube at rapid speed for eventual collision, and measuring the tragedy awaiting the poor little particles. Apparently the speed of the atoms, if I recall correctly (and if I do not, no one reading this book will know), could be controlled by a knob on the device.

What these two young scientists had built, however, was an extra knob. The Chef's Knob, as they called it, was designed for use by their faculty advisor, who would come in with some regularity to make his mark, set things straight, and generally help out. He was the Chief, the Chef, the Guy in Charge. What he didn't know at the time was that the Chef's Knob was not connected to anything. His two young protégés would "ooh" and "ahh" at the "improvements" made when their professor tweaked the Chef's Knob, knowing full well that either nothing was happening, or that what did happen was only because one of them was dialing the real knob. The Chef's Knob was for show. It was for keeping the guy at the top in the loop but out of the soup. Sounds kind of like noses in, elbows out, right?

Organizations going through significant change must manage every step of that change very carefully. It is not the job for the board. Good CEO relations depend on directors knowing that. Tone at the top, as I've discussed, starts at the board.

But driving change? Turning the knob of just how and how fast change is managed? No.

Knowing What the Organization Can Handle

It *is* the board's role to prepare the organization for change, especially in advance of a CEO change. It is also the board's role to prepare a new CEO for the culture she is stepping into, and for being there to help as the CEO turns the "real knob" of change.

Different industries have different requirements for change. Acquiring a tech firm and expecting to move at a slower and more deliberate pace than your predecessor? Do so and your lunch will be eaten in short order by a competitor who is more fleet of foot. Also, different employee bases have different appetites for change. Planning for change at a big bureaucracy that is dependent on large staffs of long-time workers? Take it slow and easy.

Different owner structures also have different change values. I worked at two global enterprises competing with labor in South America and Asia. Our profitability depended on controlling our labor costs. Unfortunately, this required moving out of communities where we had operated for years, and it cost many jobs. Had we been family-owned instead of publicly traded, we might have made different decisions about those changes. But as a public company, our shareholders valued quarterly earning more than maintaining goodwill in the community. Presumably, you have a CEO who understands those differences. You must be a resource and guide to them as they, not you, drive the pace of change. As they do their job, however, it is helpful for you to appreciate the landmines they must navigate.

Building a Culture of Change

The reality is there are an infinite number of reasons executives make changes. But one of the biggest is compensation. Compensation, in fact, is the cause for some of the biggest battles in corporate governance. The battle lines are not limited to the CEO and the board or to the CEO and the C-suite. Executive compensation is on the radar screen of just about every stakeholder companies have. That is why managing it well is the seventh imperative in the framework for Corporate Concinnity in the boardroom.

A New Framework for Governing

#1 Draw a Line in the Sand

#2 Don't Go Overboard

#3 Assemble at the Same Starting Blocks

#4 Mind the Stakeholder Gap

#5 Manage Your Information Appetite

#6 Be Prepared: Culture and Change Readiness

#7 Don't Leave Compensation to the Experts

#8 Bench Your Inner Coach

#9 Off-Board Well

#10 Cultivate Wisdom

Don't Leave Compensation to the Experts

> Do your job and demand your compensation—but in
> that order. — CARY GRANT

COMPENSATION IS AMONG the hottest topics in corporate governance, and getting it right is critical for concinnity, although probably not for the reasons you think. Nor is going about it the recommended way always the best approach.

It is important to get CEO and executive compensation just right; it is a great tool to attract, retain, and properly motivate exceptional talent. But it is more than that; proper compensation is elemental for good board-CEO relations, good board-shareholder relations, good CEO-shareholder relations, good CEO-employees relations, and, frankly, better relationships between all of the players in the governance game and all their stakeholders.

As I mentioned, executive comp is on everybody's radar screen. It's kind of like being pregnant; all of a sudden you are public property. Everyone in the world has some advice or suggestion, even people on the elevator you don't know from Adam's housecat. Executive comp is one of the highest-profile actions boards and executives must get right, together. I am a big fan of getting the best advice money can buy in this area. But I am adamant that concinnity around the issue of compensation depends on you *not* leaving comp to the experts. Doing so is one of the most common mistakes in governance, and it leads to trouble for companies and players. But let's talk first about how best to use experts.

Get Great Professional Help

The first thing to get right in compensation is to hire the right guy. To do that, you ask yourself: Whom can I call to help me find someone great? I would say that eight times out of ten you won't think, *Call a headhunter*, but rather, *Who do I know who knows a great CEO?* The arrogance of board members and investors to think they can source a CEO without enlisting the help of a service—a total Scrooge move—typically ends with companies spending more time and money. My advice to you? Stop being such a cheapskate.

I can't tell you how many otherwise intelligent, successful businesspeople become resistant when it comes to hiring a professional to nail down certain aspects of the talent side of their business, including executive search. At times it's the old cost-saving motivation. Sometimes, it's the ego saying, "I am well connected and know anybody who's anybody in this business, so how can I be more than a degree of separation from the right candidate?" Either way, it usually spells trouble for the company. There is a reason very large successful companies hire one of the top four or six search firms, or their boutique counterparts, for filling important roles. These providers have a professional skill set that the companies need to tap into.

But let's say you are feeling generous. You are going to do the right thing and hire some professional help. Before you feel too good about yourself, let me—as a former search executive—take my privilege of criticizing within the family. In the search and staffing business, the barriers to entry are extremely low. Got some time on your hands? Go into the search business. Got some friends with great skill sets? Go into the placement business. Have an appetite for selling? Go into the search or staffing business! Supply is huge. Not all search professionals are created equal. How do you choose? Again, I can't count on four hands the number of clients I have had whose desire to save a five-figure sum prevented them from hiring the best qualified team to find them someone who would handle millions of dollars for their company. If you are going to use professionals, and you're at this stage of the game when you could use them, then get the best person you can for your company. This doesn't have to mean hiring one of the big four, but it does mean getting a professional who will become your consultant in this process.

This individual will be invaluable in obtaining comparable compensation information, which comes with the cost of the search. They also provide invaluable consulting to the C-suite team into which your CEO will be placed. A good examination of the C-suite will clarify needs and become a part of the "selling" of the company to your future CEO. This work is a wonderful companion piece to the organizational assessment. It drills down to the individual roles of the players and results in a great job description and great performance metrics, which can be the basis of incentive compensation. A good executive search professional has deep expertise and data on both.

C-Suite Talent and Comp

Your relationship with your CEO is a close second to the one she will build with her C-suite. These are the folks who will make it happen for the company. Unless you have plans for changing out more of the senior leadership team than just the CEO, assessing this team of individuals is important in determining what additional resources will be needed and when to get where the company needs to go[26]. What you are looking for in your next CEO should be dependent on the talent in the C-suite that needs to be matched, balanced, augmented, and complemented. Think of the CEO hire as filling out the senior leadership team (again, unless there are problems you know you need to address with other placements in the C-suite). If you are not sure, the evaluation process that I recommend as your search firm's first consulting component will ferret that out. In building out the C-suite in a new or transformed situation or in the case of departure of a senior executive, honesty about the present strengths and weaknesses of the existing team is critical. If this is too difficult or requires a negative focus on weaknesses, then at least look at the skills and contributions resident in the C-suite compared with the skills and contributions needed to deliver on the strategy, and define the gap. Again, honesty is paramount. Often the team is honest but not self-aware, as a team or as individuals. This can happen for a variety of reasons; for starters, everyone has a stake in the outcome. It takes a very mature leadership team and a very mature governance structure (read: not usually in the first two to four years of new investor

....

26 If you know you need to make greater changes in the whole C-suite, an even more comprehensive assessment of the leadership team will be in order— get an advisor!

ownership!) to be able to work openly through this sort of gap analysis. This is where an independent advisor can be worth his or her weight in gold, because the advisor's only concern is the success of the enterprise.

Further, an advisor can assess compensation all across the C-suite. A fundamental principle of concinnity is internal equity of compensation among the members of a team who must work together more closely than anyone else. If you are a public company, everyone will know the CEO's compensation—that's one of the great things about public-company CEO salaries. People don't have to wonder, and if you get it right, it won't generate ill will. When people do have to wonder, they worry, they get jealous, and they have self-doubt. All those feelings contribute to a sense of destructive competition within the team that must pull together, not against themselves. Do yourself and the company a favor: establish a good compensation structure and program for the whole C-suite.

The best search professionals will be able to advise you on setting initial compensation. At a minimum they should provide you with comparable base, cash bonus, and long-term or stock awards by industry, company size, and geography. The following chart is an example of what you should be looking for.

Be careful to look at the three types of comps separately. As in other areas, where you are going is more important than where you are now. Trying to grow a young company fast? You will want an executive who has done that before and is, therefore, now working for a larger company. So, small-company salaries may not be appropriate for that candidate. Are you running your company in the wilds by your favorite fishing hole because that's where you want to live, where someone wanted to live at some

JOB TITLE	SURVEY SOURCE	SURVEY AGE	COMPANY SIZE AND INDUSTRY	BASE PAY*			TOTAL CASH COMP*			SURVEY WEIGHT	TARGET TOTAL CASH COMP**		
				P25	P50	P75	P25	P50	P75		P25	P50	P75
CEO			Media Rev. $10M–$50M	228.6	299.2	388.1	314.2	482.0	753.8	30%	94.3	144.6	226.1
			Healthcare Rev. $10M–$50M	177.8	232.7	301.8	244.3	374.8	586.2	30%	73.3	112.4	175.9
			Rev. $30M SIC 2730	241.6	322.1	426.6	300.8	400.9	531.0	20%	60.2	80.2	106.2
			Rev. $30M SIC 8000	192.2	282.1	399.0	239.6	351.7	497.4	20%	47.9	70.3	99.5
			Average	210.1	284.0	378.9	274.7	402.4	592.1		275.6	407.6	607.7
			Nat'l								344.5	509.5	759.6
			Local								248.1	366.8	546.9
CFO			Media Rev. $10M–$50M	174.5	222.2	279.9	225.5	321.4	464.6	30%	67.7	96.4	139.4
			Healthcare Rev. $10M–$50M	158.9	202.2	254.7	205.1	292.1	422.2	30%	61.5	87.6	126.7
			Rev. $30M SIC 2730	167.8	214.6	275.3	188.1	240.5	308.6	20%	37.6	72.2	92.6
			Rev. $30M SIC 8000	144.6	191.4	252.2	158.0	209.1	275.6	20%	31.6	62.7	82.7
			Average	161.5	207.6	265.5	194.2	265.8	367.8	100%	198.4	318.9	441.3
			Nat'l								248.0	398.7	551.6
			Local								178.6	287.0	397.2

Salaries are in hundreds of thousands.   * P equals percentile   ** Factors Survey Age, Industry, Size time, or where you find cheap labor? Recruiting a top-notch CEO to the boondocks may actually require more compensation, so be careful how you use geographic comps. Industry comps also have pitfalls, often because your company is not a pure industry play, or at least not represented by the standard data. In this chart there are four different salary surveys, representing slightly different industries and a range of sizes. Each survey is weighted to produce a composite average. Once you have the right composite average you must decide which percentile makes sense for your company. Should you be paying at the top of the range— the seventy-fifth percentile and above—to recruit and retain, or do you need room to grow and feel the twenty-fifth percentile is appropriate? This data is critical, but it is only the starting point for your good thinking applied to the situation. Notice that this chart includes comparables for the CEO and the CFO. Having this data allows you to determine if you have appropriate relationships between salaries among the C-suite's key players.

Equity Compensation

The compensation chart does not address a major component of compensation: stock. There is ample data on that, and you will want to get it if you are public or even if you are a private company. If you are recruiting a CEO, equity compensation is not only expected, it is an excellent way to align the interests of shareholders and management. If you are family-owned and have not allowed ownership outside of the family before, you should seek expert advice on how to do that, either through a change in policy or through the development of what is referred to as phantom stock, or faux options. These "securities," as they're called, perform like real stock, so they accomplish alignment of CEO interests to owner interests without having to give ownership away. The device gives the executive all the financial benefits of increases in stock valuation.

A Word about Perquisites . . .

Salary surveys show that perks are becoming more and more rare as a part of executive comp. Gone are the days of golf club memberships, planes, cars, and other luxuries.

That's not all bad. One result of their decline has been increased shareholder satisfaction with executive comp. The reality is that most folks just don't think perks are fair: not for those paying them (the shareholders), or for those who don't get them. It would appear that they often caused more trouble than they were worth.

There is one executive benefit, however, that should *not* go the way of the dinosaur. It is not even called a perk in many circumstances, but I mention it here because it is a crucial element of the whole packet you offer your CEO: executive mentoring.

An Ongoing Challenge

Once you have recruited the greatest CEO since sliced bread, keeping her compensation in line will be an ongoing activity. As I mentioned, it is among the hottest topics in governance circles and a common grievance of the activist-investor. Getting CEO comp right is the board's job: set it too low, and you will have problems recruiting and retaining; Set it too high, and you will have shareholder problems, employee morale problems, and a CEO who has a problem with her stakeholders. So get the information you need on an ongoing basis and think hard about it. Most companies feel they have fair compensation systems, and at some level they do; getting good outside help is a big part of that. But the board needs to own compensation decisions for the CEO and the C-suite.

Leaving Compensation to the Experts

I was talking to a board member friend recently about board committees. He said, "Anyone could serve on the compensation committee, because comp is always left to the experts. Any comp committee worth its salt would hire comp consultants, who would tell the board how to compensate the CEO."

Really? I agree that board compensation committees should engage consultants if they are financially able to do so, or consult a good search executive if they are not. Many small-cap companies are tight on consulting dollars, and many private equity owners feel as if they have enough knowledge within their ranks and/or portfolio of companies that they don't need consultants. To them I would say, *always* find a friendly search executive who can provide you with market, size, and geographic salary comps. But leave compensation solely to the experts? Not on your life.

Good compensation planning begins with the end in mind, meaning the end of the relationship with the executive. It goes without saying that you want to consider other ends: where you want the executive to take the company, how those goals will be measured, and how that will determine compensation. But it is also critical to consider the other "end." Relationships between CEOs and companies always come to an end. Even with family members, and even with founders. Boards must plan for this.

High-profile battles between boards and CEOs seem to

be the norm these days. One in particular, a case study in failing to think about the end, dominated the press a couple of years ago. The company was a major retailer, owned largely by a few private equity firms. It was a classic case of a founder/CEO who had become so entrenched that lines of demarcation between his personal life and professional life had become quite blurred. But that was only part of the problem. Tales of personal impropriety finally brought things to a head. Unfortunately, the departure of the CEO was a condition of default on the company's financial obligations. This meant that the company's ability to continue as a going concern hung in the balance.

As a former banker myself, I am aware of how critical it is to keep a company in the hands of a trusted CEO. I was big on key man life insurance[27] for all of my middle market clients to protect the company's interests in the event of a death. Death is unpredictable. But departure as a condition of default? Was the company bereft of keys to the kingdom of success without this guy? A company of this size had no more bench strength than that? One can presume it didn't, given the default clause concerning his departure. One has to wonder which experts advised this. Did the board know that this was a condition of default on the company's obligations? Arguably, with the high

....

27   This is a life insurance policy that a company purchases on a key executive's life. The company is the beneficiary of the plan and pays the insurance policy premiums. It's also known as "key man insurance," "key woman insurance," or "business life insurance." Key person insurance is needed if the sudden loss of a key executive would have a large negative effect on the company's operations. The payout provided from the death of the executive essentially buys the company time to find a new person or to implement other strategies to save the business.

rate of CEO turnover, it should not have been. Sure, this guy was a founder, but even founders depart. This must be considered as part of compensation planning.

How do companies get themselves into that situation? By leaving the compensation solely to the experts and by failing to plan for departures. One of my own clients presented a case where I was again left scratching my head about which "experts" came up with the compensation plan. The board was concerned about the senior leadership team, but the CEO was the clear problem, both from a performance and a personal perspective. As it turned out, my client's CEO had become quite entrenched, just like the high-profile CEO in the previous anecdote. Our findings showed serious problems with the CEO, so we asked to see his employment contract.

In my entire career, I could only have dreamed of having such a contract. The guy practically had to gun down the entire board in order to be justly terminated. In lieu of such a black swan event, the company would be required to make payments that would be damaging to its bottom line over multiple quarters. Who came up with that? The experts, no doubt. One has to wonder how often the experts are selected or engaged by the CEOs themselves. This is not an area you want to delegate to management. I've seen it done in private companies all too often.

So please, do yourself a favor and don't leave comp to the experts. Better that the board should think of the experts' advice and the comparable data as a starting point. The process should include a screen for validating or invalidating recommendations. Things to consider include short-term incentive validity, long-term incentive validity, performance-based comp, alignment with shareholder interests, clawbacks, deferred compensation, and benefits. And then the board should do a gut check, a smell test, a reasonableness check. Ask yourselves: Where could this go wrong, either in failing to properly motivate/retain or hold accountable the executive in question? How and when could this blow up, and then where would we be? The reality is that every CEO will depart; it's just a question of when . . . and how.

There are other, less obvious reasons why you don't want to leave the board's comp decisions to the experts. For one thing, experts don't believe they are paid to be creative. For another, they don't know your company as well as you do. And they may be behind the curve in times of quickly moving shareholder or other stakeholder opinion.

Recently I heard a panel of experts speak on executive compensation. While I don't remember the particulars of what they were recommending, I do recall quite a list of things to avoid, most of them related to the top five issues of the most vocal proxy advisor firms. I had been personally very interested in the Whole Foods CEO salary cap (at a max multiple of the lowest employee), something that few companies were doing at that time. So I asked one of the experts whether Whole Foods was truly an outlier or the beginning of a trend. I had barely finished asking my question when the responder dismissed the Whole Foods case as less than mildly relevant. I accepted her opinion; but then, less than six months later, such caps were on the list of top ten comp issues to watch for all boards. Was this expert wrong? Perhaps not, in her narrow universe.

The off-base bias is a particular compensation risk for board members who are currently, or in past lives have been, very highly compensated executives. It is a particular hazard for not-for-profit or small-company board directors. It is important to remember that your personal experience is often not necessarily relevant to the CEO of the company you serve as board director.

Insider Biases and Egos

I was on the board of a not-for-profit that was struggling to keep salaries rising, something many members presumed we must do, despite a period of high unemployment and very low inflation. A couple of successful business people on the board were concerned with what we were paying our senior team, in particular. To them the salaries seemed low. These board members had been senior executives or CEOs of much larger companies. Their personal compensation experience had been different. While their intentions were in the right place, their perspective came from a very different context. In reality, for an organization of that not-for-profit's size, geography, and industry, the salaries were in line. They might have been low for another industry, but not for ours and not in the bigger picture. We board members must always be aware of our biases as we bring our expertise to the table.

Unless compensation is rightsized for the company in good times and in bad, with a balance of accountability, motivation, and retention, it will come to a head 100 percent of the time. Someone is going to howl. When that happens, the program must be valid enough to withstand those challenges. It must be flexible enough to be refitted to the circumstances and the people.

Comp Expertise . . . As Needed

Few issues are bigger potential lightning rods for company stakeholders than executive compensation. Activist investors may be leading the charge on CEO compensation rationalization or justification, but they have an army of troops at their back. Getting it right is fundamental to building concinnity in the boardroom and constructive harmony among stakeholders. It's also key to attracting and retaining exceptional talent: the kind of talent that will build sustainability in leadership that is equally fundamental to high performance.

Directors must satisfy themselves that they are receiving wise advice and counsel from experts who are armed with the latest data and thinking. But then they must take that information under advisement as they seek to check their collective gut that the recommendations are rightsized for the company, both as it is and where it is going. Leaving comp to the experts not only abrogates one of the board's most important responsibilities, it actually increases the chance that you will not get compensation right.

So, my final message: Leave the compensation to the experts? Only if you want to lose your CEO or the goodwill of other stakeholders.

Each executive brings a wealth of knowledge and experiences to the roles he or she plays. If the process has been well managed by all involved, the executive will be an exceptional match. But no one is perfect. Even if you have worked hard and found in one package someone who has accomplished the tasks at hand and has the cultural fit, they will not be perfect. They will have blind spots, just like every other human.

Identifying blind spots in advance by yourself is difficult, if not impossible. One reason the average tenure of executives in the C-suite is so short is that boards don't plan for challenges. The best insurance against CEO failure is augmenting the executive with an executive guide: Imperative 8 in building Corporate Concinnity.

A New Framework for Governing

#1 Draw a Line in the Sand

#2 Don't Go Overboard

#3 Assemble at the Same Starting Blocks

#4 Mind the Stakeholder Gap

#5 Manage Your Information Appetite

#6 Be Prepared: Culture and Change Readiness

#7 Don't Leave Compensation to the Experts

#8 Bench Your Inner Coach

#9 Off-Board Well

#10 Cultivate Wisdom

Bench Your Inner Coach

> Everyone needs a coach. It doesn't matter whether you're
> a basketball player, a tennis player, a gymnast, or a bridge
> player. —BILL GATES

YOU'VE PROBABLY HEARD the tale of the blind men and the elephant. The men gather around the elephant to touch it and describe what it is. One man touches the trunk and he feels a "hose," while another touches the tail and he feels a "cord." Still another is checking out a leg and a foot and announces, "It is a tree." Which one was right? They all were; there was nothing incorrect in what they described. Each description was, however, incomplete. The point of the story is that you can't see what you don't know. Likewise, you don't know what you can't see.

Understanding Their Need and Your Role

Corporate leaders are hired for what they are able to see: for their creativity, their energy, their expertise, and their temperament. But all have blind spots, and your CEO is no different. All CEOs—all of them—need someone to help them see what they can't see. It is a grave mistake to pretend they don't.

According to a 2013 *Forbes* survey,

1. Nearly 100 percent of CEOs **wish** they had coaching or leadership advice from *outside* consultants.[28]

2. Only one-third of them get it.

Why is that? From my experience, one of the most common culprits is the board itself.

There are two types of unsound thinking among directors that handicap the CEO and the company. Many directors, given their age, do not have personal experience with professional coaches or individual executive advisors. As a result, they carry a prejudice against them. Some know them only in a narrow sense, so they might also have a bias against them. Other directors believe in coaching and mentoring but think *they* can be the personal advisor to their CEOs. Not only does this fall short, it sets a horrible stage for conflict in governance. Board members are absolutely not the best personal advisors for their CEOs.

It is imperative that you bench your inner coach. We all have one. We didn't get to the boardroom for nothing. We are smart and successful and may have even mentored a number of senior leaders along the way. We may know *how to*, but we easily forget *when* and *when not to*. You and your CEO deserve better.

Note that according to the same *Forbes* survey, nearly 100 percent of CEOs wish they had received coaching or leadership advice *from outside of their companies*. When a CEO says "outside of the company," that includes *you*, board member. *You* are inside the company. Don't forget that you are the CEO's boss.

....
28   *Forbes Magazine*, August 5, 2013.

I have had many venture capital and private equity clients who pride themselves on what a good job they do as advisors to their portfolio company CEOs. Many of these investors promote the quality of their partners, who are former CEOs, and their operating partners as their key *differentiators*, leading to capabilities that make the color of their capital different from that of their competitors'. I am not critical of using this intelligence as a resource for CEOs. I think it is impossible to have too much intelligence in today's business world, as long as it is used soundly and given in moderation. To paraphrase my earlier chapter, you don't have to tell them everything, or even anything, that you think of!

But this kind of advice is not personal advice, nor counsel of the nature every CEO needs. Board directors can certainly be invaluable in helping CEOs think through business issues such as strategy, risk, growing the business, capital and capital markets management, and other matters that concern where a company is going and what it is facing. These are issues for the company, not the CEO.

PEER MENTORING: Peer mentors are executives who currently have or have had in their past functional roles similar to that of the mentee or client executive; they advise and counsel on how to be successful in the role. Peer mentoring often focuses on the "hard skills" aspects of the job. Peer mentors can be internal or external to the executive's company, and usually work as volunteers.

But if the CEO needs help on personal issues, the board member is too close to help. Depending on whether the matters he or she wants to focus on are soft-skill related or hard-skill related, either an executive coach or an individual executive advisor is needed. It is important to appreciate that the advice and counsel that boards can provide is no substitute for the professional advice your CEO needs.

Neither is what I call "Big Brother/Big Sister Mentoring." A lot of people I talk to tell me how many wonderful mentors they've had in their careers, how they have always made it a priority to reach out to more senior people for advice and counsel. I don't doubt the virtue of this. I have benefitted from it myself. While Big Brother/Big Sister Mentoring can be quite valuable, it is not the same as retaining an executive coach or an individual executive advisor. While valuable from one standpoint, just like the advice and counsel from directors, these relations are not the same as being in a relationship with a professional.

Why Individual Executive Advising and Coaching Work

Business seems to have come late to the individual executive advising and coaching party. Somehow we think our challenges are different. The most common reasons I hear for not engaging a professional include the following:

1. Executive coaches and individual executive advisors are for failures.
2. We can or should do it ourselves.
3. We can't afford it.
4. We don't have time.
5. We can't imagine how anyone can help.
6. We think that's what all those board directors are for.[29]

....
29   Even if directors have said that, they're wrong. They're the CEO's boss.

These are terrible reasons for not hiring an individual executive advisor or coach! Still it would surprise me if you or someone you know on your board doesn't harbor some of these notions.

Let's start with coaching and individual advising are for failures. Tell that to any elite athlete and hear them laugh. Tiger Woods is arguably the best golfer of all time. How many coaches do you think he has? Do you think he hires them because he thinks he's a failure? No, he does it because he wants to stay at the top of his game. He knows something that many executives deny, which is that we all have problems, all of the time. But that doesn't make us problem children; it doesn't make us executives who are failing. Business got it wrong in the beginning. We thought of coaching as something for people who were non-performers, and that's how we used it in the beginning. We waited until executives began to show signs of failure before we called in the coaches. That history is unfortunate, because it leads to fear of asking for advice, which everyone needs.

The second notion—thinking we can or should do it ourselves—is all about ego and guilt. Think again about the blind man and the elephant. You can't see the whole picture on your own. There is probably some reasonable period of time to try to go it alone in solving a particular problem. But this is not a formula for continuous improvement in the game of executive leadership. It is the height of arrogance to think we don't need support. The guilt side of this bias can be diffused through the admission of the reality of time constraints. Leaders are firing on all cylinders and often slaying dragons in other areas, so they don't have time to help. A professional spends all her time doing this, looking at root causes and effects, diagnosing problems, connecting dots. The diagnoses alone can be powerful. They can save millions in surprisingly short order. Getting help diagnosing problems sooner is something I've never seen *not* pay off; it always proves worthwhile.

Reason 3 leads executives to think they can't afford it. CFO types are the worst; they grew up achieving organizational wins in cost-saving programs. Spending money on themselves is something they can be extremely shortsighted about, even though cost/benefit analysis is their bread and butter. Not only does it cost less than you think to get individual executive advising or coaching, the cost pales in comparison to the money you will make by being more effective. Those who think they don't have time for it just don't appreciate what it is like to have a professional work on their own schedule. My coach, who is a rock star, provided advice and counsel that was on my schedule, on demand, and enhanced my efficiency many times over. Those of us who can't imagine how anyone can help usually just don't have any experience with the profession. We are busy running companies, not working full time at making executives great.

Over an embarrassingly long chunk of one summer, I had my fairway wood in "time-out." I could not get that thing to perform for me. I even took a new fairway wood out for a test drive, thinking it *had* to be the club. My last resort was to book thirty minutes with the pro to work on the offending club's performance. It probably took two seconds for her to figure out what I was doing wrong. Honest to goodness, it was like a miracle. All of a sudden, that darned club was like magic, saving me at least one stroke on those painful par-five holes. Sure, I still needed practice and some continued trial and error to make the new swing mine and sustain the improvement. But the diagnosis was not only extremely powerful, it was necessary. And more to the point, I couldn't imagine the change; I couldn't imagine the result. I was obsessed with conquering it on my own with what I knew. That was my big mistake.

My pro is a pretty smart cookie. She can see when I get frustrated that I am not improving with parts of my game. She gave me a great analogy. "Look at what you do and what I do," she said. "Suppose you gave me a complex spreadsheet to analyze. How many of those a day do you work on? How many do I? I would never expect myself to do what you can do!" She coached me not to expect to play like a pro—not with my time on the course or the range. If you play golf, have you ever had a lesson? Were you amazed at its effectiveness? Have you ever been sick, and gone to the doctor? Were you surprised at the diagnosis and impressed at how quickly the complaint went away? In the same way, executive coaching is not for the remedial learner or for the fainthearted. Like coaches engaged by elite athletes, they are invaluable for making the good great.

Why Individual Executive Advising and Coaching Work

> **EXECUTIVE COACHING:** Executive coaches are professionals who are engaged by executives and/or their companies for the purpose of enhancing performance. Many executive coaches have backgrounds in psychology and are able to use that expertise in matters of personal effectiveness, interpersonal relations, general leadership, and a variety of other "soft skills."

Discipline. CEOs are, by and large, very disciplined people. But the focus of their discipline is on the performance of the company and that of other people in it: a very demanding and time-consuming responsibility. It often leads to a lack of discipline in self-care and improvement. Being in a relationship with a professional is the only way to cut through other demands and make the executive's own performance improvement a priority. It just won't happen otherwise. And with that discipline comes repetition.

Repetition. Undoubtedly, CEOs work with coaches on complex problems. They require repeated efforts to resolve. Repetition is hard without coaches. If you don't believe me, how many people do you see in the gym doing serious reps without a personal trainer hovering over them? But repetition works, mentally as well as physically. When I was living in the New York area, I listened to the main news radio station. They had an hourly update on the news that started with something like, "Give us ten minutes, we'll give you the world." I listened to it daily. If I was driving around, I heard it a lot—like ten minutes every hour. That meant that every hour I was getting much the same news! I can still recall vividly the accompanying, old-fashioned teletype sound that went along with the broadcast and specific events reported far better than those that happened in other times of my life. Repetition is a powerful thing. I know a music instructor who says to his students, "Repetition is the mother of learning." You'd better believe it.

Perspective. In addition to discipline and repetition, individual executive advisors and coaches bring a perspective that is impossible to see otherwise. Sometimes they bring it from their own experiences; other times they are incredibly deft at channeling new observations in their clients as they engage in joint reflection of events. The added element of reflection also ensures that the repetition is of activities that the executive is supposed to be focused on.

Reflection. The problem is that most of us have an incredibly hard time sticking to the program of routine and reflection, and when we do reflect it happens in the vacuum of our own minds, without additional, necessary context and perspective. The reflection is informed, but only by our own expertise and experiences. Great leaders are generally self-aware, and self-awareness is a critical element in self-improvement. But once we get into positions of very senior leadership, others stop giving us perspective. Their jobs are generally to get done what we set in motion. What this means is that subordinates are spending time making the boss happy, not giving the boss constructive feedback. From the boss's perspective, that can cut out a lot of constructive input that even the most self-aware leaders need. Inasmuch as we only know what we know, unguided reflection is less effective. Routine is important, reflection is key, but partnering with an independent, trusted advisor is necessary for all the discipline and consideration to produce the results needed to make execs perform at the top of their game and, as a consequence, for companies to meet or exceed their performance expectations.

Confidentiality. A well-selected individual executive advisor brings to the table complementary experiences, expertise, and confidentiality. The ones that have already been there and done that, or done something very approximate. And a good individual executive advisor can provide a safe space to discuss sensitive topics, be they one's own weaknesses or politically sensitive issues.

> **INDIVIDUAL EXECUTIVE ADVISING:** Individual executive advisors are a hybrid between executive coaches and peer mentors. Many individual executive advisors come out of the C-suite and as such have track records of success in both the hard skills and soft skills required for the job of the client executive. Individual executive advisors are external to the client's company and are paid.

I have written before about the importance of candor from the top, even when—especially when—there is uncertainty that can introduce excessive fear into the company culture and dramatically impact performance. There is a right and wrong way to be transparent in these situations. Having an individual executive advisor to think through just how to execute this is very valuable. And there are some topics that senior executives need to share and talk through with someone that really cannot be shared within the company. It is far more effective and less disruptive to culture and morale to work through alternatives with the advice and counsel of a dedicated individual executive advisor.

Convenience. CEOs are among the busiest people in the world. Effective use of their time is the only way they can be successful. A personal, executive advisor delivers just what they need, when and how they need it. It is up to you, as the boss of the CEO, and the C-suite indirectly, to make sure there are means outside your company to find those advisors who have the experience and expertise that are a custom fit for where your CEO and others in the C-suite are, and for what they have to do. These professionals have to be capable of serving the advising up to your executives on their timetable and schedule: if you will, on a silver platter. Consider how my own MBA program was delivered to me.

I was commuting to New York City one day on the New Haven line, and the only available seat was in that short-car section at the end of the train. There were a number of people in the front of that little section, but I found a spot hidden in the back. As the train was pulling out of the station I adjusted my coffee and cruller and opened my *Wall Street Journal* to settle into a quiet forty-five minutes of catching up on the business news. Or so I thought. Within minutes the strangest-looking portable white board was opened up and attached to the railing in front of the exit doors area. With that, a senior-looking business executive was up on his feet, and commenced speaking about a business school case.

I had wandered into an MBA class that was being taught on the commuter train, Adelphi University's MBA on Wheels Program, to be exact. My eyes got as big as saucers. *You can do this?* When I made the move to the New York area, I had made the decision to stay in banking rather than pursue a full-time MBA, which was something I knew I needed. What Adelphi was offering me was a way to get my MBA while doing something I had to do anyway: commute to work. It was like an MBA program brought to me by room service.

I was on the phone to the school before that day was over, and within a couple of years I had earned my MBA. It was astounding: my learning and content needs delivered on my schedule and my timetable. The programming was high quality, the professors exceptional, and my fellow students contributed immeasurably to my business learning. But none of that would have worked for me had I not had it all available precisely on my schedule.

By the time people get to the C-suite, they have a lot on their plates, many balls to juggle, and many competing demands. They know they must keep learning to be at the top of their game. They have no peers in their company, no one who has been there and done that in terms of what the company is calling on them to do—unlike in their early years when they had mentors with many more years' experience. But the need for that mentoring doesn't stop just because one rises to the level of his or her former mentors.

The good news is that it is there for you and them. And it probably doesn't require the investment of time and money that you think it does. The fact that it is customized, structured, and scheduled in a tailored manner means that the coaching will be far more efficient and effective than any other manner of getting advice and counsel. Your executives will find themselves more motivated as they seek to be accountable to their advisor, and more effective as they get wise counsel on both hard- and soft-skill topics. In addition they will find themselves enjoying their work and its challenges more.[30]

Boardroom Coaching

I was advising a particular board on matters of organization and governance process. Several members of the board felt that its work was not being conducted in an efficient manner. As a result of poor agendas, insufficient minutes, and lack of

....

30 So where can the board go to find this for the C-suite? The Concinnity Company (theconcinnitycompany.com) provides advisory services for companies, their boards, and their leadership teams, including one-on-one and team executive coaching and individual executive advising.

follow-through, the board was not able to achieve what it set out to do over the course of the year. After interviewing several members of the board, it was clear that the board chairwoman was the roadblock.

The other directors felt she could not get sufficiently organized to tend to the administrative aspects of her role. I knew her well enough to know that she was incredibly smart, in addition to being passionate about and committed to the mission of the organization. Still, I went into this situation with a bias, informed by others I had interviewed, that she did not know what she was supposed to be doing and/or was not well organized enough to do it.

The other directors were not entirely correct. The chairwoman's issue was values-related. She did not think she was particularly on top of the administrative side of things, but she didn't see that the administrative and organizational tasks involved in her particular role were all that important. The disconnect arose because others saw them as crucial and not getting done, while she felt they were something of low value. As a result, the board's work was inefficient, tasks took far longer than they should have, and people were frustrated. It didn't have to be this way, and once all of the opinions were laid out on the table, they were resolved and the board's work improved. At the same time, the director's enjoyment of her work also improved.

There is another lesson here: how the board worked as a team, how it communicated with one another, and how it addressed its effectiveness as a group. Initially the board had engaged in a classic triangulation. I had multiple conversations with the chair's colleagues about what bothered them, but they had not communicated to her directly—at least not in a way that made a difference. They might say they did and that she did not get it or address it. She might say they didn't. Either way, good governance is a team sport, so they all failed.

I think every executive should enlist a coach's advice on some sort of regular basis. A board must also engage someone to advise it about how it works as a group. The one-on-one work we do with our coaches usually relates to enhancing our full-time work, but we need to be at the top of our game in the boardroom as well.

Board consultants can be invaluable in helping boards function as teams. Board consultants typically conduct some sort of 360-degree evaluation, where everyone is surveyed on topical and general governance matters, as opposed to personal qualities. The surveys often reveal issues such as, "We are not planning our meetings well." The board member responsible for that will receive constructive information, and by working as a team, with or without the consultants, improvements can be made. And even though the evaluations don't often take on the issue of individual work, they can.

Someone from outside the company and outside the board can be the catalyst for continuous improvement for a board that regularly looks at how it is doing and works well as a team. And when they do, modulating and listening will be valuable practices.

Is Anyone Really Uncoachable?

I recently spoke with a board member of an early-stage company who mentioned that his CEO was "uncoachable." The board member, a successful executive in his own right, had much to contribute to any early-stage company CEO. Certainly in this case, he had years of success and experience that his CEO had yet to enjoy. The situation was frustrating to the board member, so he sought a retired, successful CEO from the industry to coach the CEO. That was, it would seem, beginning to bear fruit. Having communicated all that to me, this board member closed our conversation by remarking again that his CEO was uncoachable.

Is there such a thing as a CEO who is, in fact, not coachable? People seem to hold especially fast to first impressions when considering character and leadership traits of colleagues. Boards need to be aware of this as their CEOs work with coaches. Research also shows that acceptance of leadership change and progress increases when three things happen: 1) stakeholders are engaged in defining the traits that need to be changed, 2) plans for making change are communicated, and 3) self-perceived progress on change goals is shared and communication about how that progress is being perceived is authentically requested, also known as "feed-forward."[31] In the case of the executive of this early-stage company, it was not clear that he had been given the benefit of those three things. It is not wise to give up on someone before this has happened. Once you have given your CEO all the benefit of the best kind of coaching possible and things are still not working, it might be possible that the CEO's time to contribute has come to an end. But before you take action on that, I would have you consider one other thing: Is there a language barrier between the board and the CEO?

....

31 Feed-forward, a term used by Avraham Kluger and Marshall Goldsmith, involves sharing self-perceived progress on change goals and authentically asking for communication about how that progress is being perceived. It is worth noting that when asking for ideas of how to change in the feed-forward stage, all suggestions must be in the context of future action. No grousing about past sins is allowed.

I am a big fan of John Gray's book, *Men Are from Mars, Women Are from Venus*. Gray has written several books, so you've likely been exposed to one or more. I will let you decide if executives are from Venus and board directors are from Mars, or the other way around. The point is, the very role you are playing—governing or leading, directing from the board, or managing from the C-suite—heavily influences your "language," your perceptions. What Gray's book did for communication between women and men was to bring the misunderstandings out in the open. Openly acknowledged, the divergent perceptions could then be examined and result in understanding, if not resolution. Judgment was more easily suspended, and offense less often taken.

So, is there really an "uncoachable" type? Before coming to this conclusion, formalized coaching must have taken place. Remember, coaching is for the elite executive, not the remedial player. It is intended to enhance, not fix. But, if there are issues that require fixing, the board may need to put them on the table with the executive and/or the coach. Before deciding someone is not coachable, the potentiality that different languages are the real barrier to change must be considered carefully. It may also be considered with the coach. If, after all of this, the situation is not resolved, if an executive changes words but not actions, a change may be in order.

Trade your Inner Coach for a Pro

Bench your inner coach. Engage a pro for your CEO and a professional for the board itself. You, your CEO, and all of your stakeholders will be glad you did.

A New Framework for Governing

#1 Draw a Line in the Sand

#2 Don't Go Overboard

#3 Assemble at the Same Starting Blocks

#4 Mind the Stakeholder Gap

#5 Manage Your Information Appetite

#6 Be Prepared: Culture and Change Readiness

#7 Don't Leave Compensation to the Experts

#8 Bench Your Inner Coach

#9 Off-Board Well

#10 Cultivate Wisdom

Off-Board Well

Parting is such sweet sorrow that I shall say goodnight till
it be morrow. —WILLIAM SHAKESPEARE

THE CEO OF a company with whom I worked as a board advisor taught me one of my favorite aphorisms. It goes something
like this:

> When I was a young man I thought life was
> a sprint. When I got older, I figured out that
> life was in fact a marathon. I believed that for
> a long while, and then when I became wise,
> I realized that life was neither a race nor a
> marathon. Life was really a relay.

All executives have particular gifts and skills that can be
incredibly valuable to our companies in certain periods of time.
But these days, individual roles and responsibilities, if not the
companies themselves, seem to change more rapidly than individuals. Companies, boards, and CEOs are behind in their
thinking on dealing with this.

The reality is that there is more than enough work in the world to which a skilled individual can contribute. Leaving doesn't have to be bad. But it will be unless the inevitable departures are handled better. This may be just one of my ten imperatives, but failing to manage departures well—off-boarding poorly—may contribute just as much as any other bad practice to creating disharmony (the opposite of concinnity) in corporate governance. You will face departures as a board member. Your CEO will face them with regularity. Deal with them appropriately.

This Was Never Going to Be Easy, but It Doesn't Have to Be Bad

Ever have one of your star performers get a once-in-a-lifetime opportunity? Of course you have. You could see the advantages for her, but where was the love? The loyalty? There was so much more for her to do at your company! Or have you ever had one of your favorite leaders really struggle to hit his numbers? You had felt for some time that the skills and experiences he brought to the table were no longer what the company needed—not what it really required at that particular point in time. So you needed to take action. Of course you've been there. It was not going to be easy. But it didn't have to be bad.

Our job as leaders is to be ever vigilant in keeping talent at its highest and best use. Are leaders giving us their hard-earned skills and more than our fair share of their time and lives? We can and should show gratitude for that, even when the time comes for a change. I have at times seen companies find room for a particular leader whose current role is no longer right for them or the company. This can work, but it is quite hard, especially for smaller companies or when the executive has reached very senior levels. When it won't work, our job as leaders is to take what will not be easy and make sure it is not bad.

What does a bad departure look like? We have all heard about those filled with drama and rancor. An executive is taken out in handcuffs by uniformed officers. An employee is escorted out by security.

But not all bad departures are this dramatic. Consider this: Any departure that results in the severing of a relationship with the outgoing employee is a bad departure. This includes departures where the individual is not accorded the consideration of farewells with colleagues or given the ability to make an orderly physical transition out (including dealing with personal effects.)

I am aware that boards are not personally responsible for departures, and that departments like human resources generally manage these. The fact remains that when they are managed badly, it is a very negative experience for culture and for Corporate Concinnity. After all, Corporate Concinnity is about exceptional relationships. Checking basic human kindness, dignity, and consideration at the door for an exit conversation is no way to accomplish this. It speaks volumes about your culture to the departing worker, as well as to those remaining.

Bad departures leave behind damage. People within are adversely affected. Don't forget, people's feelings about another person don't change just because the color of that person's new jersey no longer matches their own. In addition, departures at the CEO level often create boardroom rifts when they are managed badly. Finally, bad departures create new enemies outside who may still be stakeholders.

The conventional wisdom is that when a company or an

executive has decided there must be a departure, their interests immediately become entirely separate from and different from one another. That invisible wall we construct is bound to make things uncomfortable. The reality is that these executives got to where they are because they are very good at a number of things, most of which we asked them to do and they did. They will go on to do great things at other companies. If we play our cards right, the relationship, the transition itself, and future beneficial business transactions will all continue to bear fruit. This can be true whether the departure is instigated by the company or by the executive.

I know an executive for whom these things are black and white. As he tells it, "Once someone has decided to leave the company, I have no more use for that person." He's wrong. He has much to gain by working on his and the company's relationship and transition with the person, whose future use to him is, no matter what he says, potentially great. His philosophy may be stark, but he is not alone in being blind to the opportunity costs of not working hard to ensure good transitions in whatever situation creates them. The reality is that love and loyalty can often be preserved if we work hard at it. And there can be significant business potential in the future.

Granted, in some situations we lose an executive to a competitor. Those situations are more difficult for us, because we are not initiating the change. But those situations can result in future goodwill and perhaps even business opportunities. When someone leaves under competitive circumstances, a painful departure multiplies the likelihood that the person will go out of his or her way to create opportunities to help the competition. There's no way an exec doesn't take a lot of intellectual capital with him or her. How would you want that to be used: for or against you? If you believe you should "Keep your friends close and your enemies closer," then you should go out of your way to make departing executives feel close. After all, they don't have to be your enemies!

CEO and executive departures happen all of the time. Therefore, we can anticipate them and plan to handle them in a way that enhances concinnity. It is helpful to think about the departures that are particularly painful and those we most often fail to anticipate. Consider the five below:

1. The Founder
2. The Turnaround Artist
3. The Patri(matri)arch
4. The Trusted Advisor
5. The Board Director

The Founder. Founders are wonderful, creative, risk-seeking individuals who drive a significant percentage of the country's economic growth. And, by and large, process and administration drive them crazy. This is not universally true, but their skills, required to launch companies and grow them past concept stage, are unique. The best founders have these skills in spades.

I have often been contacted by board members or investors looking for a change in leadership, once their company has passed a certain life stage—let's say proof of concept or being well into profitability. They are looking for things like getting a company to scale or building a platform (read: process and administration) that will accelerate or facilitate growth. I expect if you are reading this, you've been in this situation or read case studies on it. In many situations, there is a need for new talent at the top, and managing through this change with a founder CEO is not going to be easy. But it doesn't have to be bad. It is a predictable business event. Talk about it.

The Turnaround Artist. Some of you might think this phrase is an oxymoron, since the bull in the china shop–type of turnaround expert is not uncommon. I do not share that view. Companies just happen to find themselves in situations where things are changing fast, but not in the right direction—often. Some people are just great at executing turnarounds; they are worth their weight in gold. I have recruited and placed a significant number of turnaround artists. There are even subspecialties in the turnaround world, each with different technical skills, financial restructurings, operational rationalizations, and also different personality types.

When I was in the banking world, we used to say that the commercial bankers were the Golden Retrievers of the finance world, while the investment bankers were the Dobermans. You get the idea. The kind of turnaround artists whom I engaged were on the kinder, gentler side of the personality spectrum, at least in the turnaround world. Nonetheless, they tended to break some glass, if not some furniture, along the way to righting the ship. Sometimes the breaking of so much glass was needed at a particular company that the overhaul needed a series of different types of turnaround artists on the way back to health. That is one reason why the engagement of interim executives in situations like this is so effective. When interims are engaged, the role, its duration, and its conclusion are clear. The inherent communication is such that the changing of the guard is anticipated and planned for from day one, by everyone.

If you are looking for someone to create significant change in your organization and you are not engaging an interim, you need to be realistic about how many friends your executive is going to make along the way. Some CEOs actually hire tough guys to do that work for them so that the ill will created will not adhere to the CEO, but rather to the tough guy, who can be moved on after he's done. This is not a bad strategy, as long as the departure is planned for from the outset. Your turnaround player is running a relay; plan for the handoff.

The Patri(matri)arch. A strong patriarch or matriarch often leads the family business and, as such, family businesses tend to face fewer changes in leadership than do other types of companies. As a result they can be even less prepared for the change when it eventually does happen. After years of that one person being so very much in control, it is not only the rest of the company, including the board, that will have trouble planning for this change; the CEO will struggle with it as well. Sometimes that struggle turns into denial.

A good family-owned company board can play an invaluable role in planning for CEO succession. It will be important to evaluate whether or not it is time to move outside of the family and hire professional, non-family leadership. These changes can be more complicated than non-family CEO transitions because of the ownership complexity. It is also complicated by a level of emotion between the players. Boards who are independent can evaluate various aspects of the change with objectivity that the CEO, other family owners, and perhaps other family managers cannot always manage. These transitions can be an excellent time to engage outside resources skilled with this type of transition.

The Trusted Advisor. Trusted advisors who have a history with a company can be worth their weight in gold. These include, but are not limited to, attorneys, accountants, bankers, brokers, and consultants of many types. They are very big players in the governance work we execute as a team. We are accustomed to and expect a certain amount of change among the players on a team of trusted advisors. Sometimes, when they make a move from one institution to another, we may follow them. Sometimes such a move is not practical. It is very important to think about how to deal with change in these relationships.

The board itself will engage some advisors, such as the audit firm and compensation consultants. For other key advisors that the CEO or leadership hires, we can ask the right questions to ensure that management is thinking about and planning for change in them. At one time, companies' most entrenched advisors never changed, because it was just too hard or expensive. Auditors were one such example. However, new laws now require periodic changes in public company auditors. The rationale was motivated by a reduction in risk to shareholders because of the loss of objectivity entrenched advisors can experience over time. It is worth thinking about both the unplanned changes of these key corporate players, but also ones that we should perhaps think about changing. Planning for these will limit disruptions in the concinnity we are building in our governance framework.

The Board Director. Yes, board members are running a relay, too. In Imperative 2, I mentioned that a board with excessive director tenure is one of the top ten board mistakes. I made a very strong case for board tenure limits. The downsides can be minimal if director turnover is planned for in advance. Board succession planning can ensure that the company doesn't suffer unnecessary loss of institutional knowledge and that the skills and experiences of the board as a whole don't fall below what the company needs.

There are many common pitfalls in departures of CEOs, other C-suite executives, and even board members. Planning can help your board avoid many of them. Companies, leaders, and boards have a tremendous opportunity to make departures—which will be difficult—not terrible. If fact, some make a great thing out of a hard departure.

A prestigious prep school I know was facing the transition of a long-term CEO. Many did not see it coming. The CEO was so well loved and seemed to being doing such a great job that many people didn't notice that she had reached what would arguably be considered retirement age. The school went above and beyond in managing this significant change in its life. For starters, it was announced almost a year in advance. While moving academic talent in the middle of a school year is hard, many schools don't always execute such invaluably generous transition periods. The timeframe this prep school set up allowed most players time to become accustomed to the idea of the change and to make ample preparation for the absence of the current CEO. The equally early and thoughtful naming of a new CEO likewise facilitated a smooth transition in.

Beyond that, the board made the departure an occasion for celebration. Lots of "last" events were planned, giving most stakeholders an opportunity to say goodbye. The board even went so far as to ask the mayor to declare a day in honor of the leader. This was totally unnecessary, but garnered great rewards. Indeed, what it did for the outgoing CEO was overshadowed by what it did for the school. The day turned into a fabulous public relations event. This unnecessary but thoughtful action cost nothing, but created a tremendous opportunity, as did the board's whole treatment of the departure. The board took a challenging corporate life event, in this case a CEO departure, and made it great. Not all departures will turn out this well, but focusing on what would be a good departure—what is likely to create ongoing relationships and opportunities with and through the departing executive—will guide you toward better departures.

Great Boards Off-Board Well

Great boards get the importance of off-boarding well. Life really is a relay, and so is the work of players in the leadership and governance game. At any given moment, someone is departing. Getting that right is important to good governance because of the impact these departures have on those who remain and on the will (good or ill) that is sent out into the external community as a result of these inevitable departures. By handling departures well, boards can actually create opportunities—even create concinnity—in governance. Thinking about departures in this way turns conventional wisdom about departures on its ear, to the advantage of the company. At the end of the day, concinnity in corporate governance is about having and using true, not necessarily conventional, wisdom, which is Imperative 10 in Corporate Concinnity in governing.

A New Framework for Governing

#1 Draw a Line in the Sand
#2 Don't Go Overboard
#3 Assemble at the Same Starting Blocks
#4 Mind the Stakeholder Gap
#5 Manage Your Information Appetite
#6 Be Prepared: Culture and Change Readiness
#7 Don't Leave Compensation to the Experts
#8 Bench Your Inner Coach
#9 Off-Board Well
#10 Cultivate Wisdom

Cultivate Wisdom

A man living is yielding and receptive.
Dying, he is rigid and inflexible.
All things, the grass and trees:
Living, they are yielding and fragile;
Dying, they are dry and withered.

—LAO TZU

IT WAS THE summer of 1968, a time when America had exploded into open warfare against itself. Big cities were ablaze in the aftermath of Martin Luther King Jr.'s assassination and the tension was spreading into communities of all sizes and shapes.

In a small southern town, the harassment of an elderly black man by the local police was the event that brought the community to the brink of violence. The man had been thrown to the ground and his purchases scattered, for no apparent—or at least justifiable—reason. The man's outraged community gathered in the high school gymnasium to plan their response. Anger was in the air, coiling ever tighter for release by the riot-inclined crowd.

A middle-aged white man entered the packed building—alone. He was not large in physical terms, but the mayor's presence silenced the crowd as he walked up on the stage. He asked the injured man to tell his story. Upon hearing it, Mayor Harold reached into his back pocket, pulled out his wallet, and counted out bills totaling the value of the old man's groceries. Having done this, he proclaimed to the man and the crowd, "I know this is not what you want, but it is rightfully yours. I know what you want is justice, and you have my word that you will have it."

The crowd, so certain only moments ago that it would be taking its anger from the gym to the streets, felt its mood travel instead from furor to calm. From the silenced gym, folks slowly returned to their homes.

I was told this story through the eyes of a twelve-year-old African American who was, during this same period, in the process of growing up in an all-black world. As he retold the story some forty years later, he could still feel the anger washing over him and hear the proverbial pin drop on the polished wood floor. *Four decades later*, the mayor's bravery, compassion, and ability to quiet the masses remained fresh in the mind of at least one witness to the incident.

Wisdom is the capacity of judging rightly in matters relating to life and conduct; soundness of judgment in the choice of means and ends; sometimes, less strictly, sound sense, esp. in practical affairs.[32] According to neuropsychologist Vivian Clayton, wisdom is made up of cognition, reflection, and compassion.[33]

....

32 Oxford English Dictionary.

33 http://www.vivianclaytonphd.com.

Defining Wisdom

Mayor Harold's story is not only remarkable, it is the essence of wisdom in action. Wisdom is a tough word to define. For many it's like the old adage about pornography: You can't define it, but you know it when you see it. Perhaps that is why it has occupied writers through countless volumes and more than two thousand years—from Lao Tzu's *Tao Te Ching* (600 BCE), to the books of prophets such as Solomon in the Bible (200 BCE), to hundreds of interpretations of those texts, to thousands of books on leadership written within the past two hundred years. Under almost any definition, Mayor Harold exhibited wisdom in handling a potentially explosive situation. He demonstrated good judgment in determining the best means to an end; clearly, he thought with great clarity about the situation and what was needed to bring peace to a community roiled with indignation. No doubt there were many alternative approaches that he, his advisors, and his colleagues considered. But, after recognizing the situation for what it was and reflecting carefully about both what was at stake and what might help calm prevail, he traveled alone into an angry crowd with the intent of bringing peace to the community. He was, arguably, following the wisdom of the *Tao* in choosing flexibility, of yielding to force rather than applying more.

Mayor Harold succeeded, in large part, because he instinctively recognized that acting wisely requires the compassion neuropsychologist Vivian Clayton claims is essential to true wisdom. In addition to making good decisions, this man clearly managed himself well and maintained the kind of mature relationship with the consequences that Clayton argues is essential—one of accepting the limits of one's control.

But how exactly did this man's actions become the embodiment of wisdom? What enabled him to silence angry masses? How was it that he touched lives in ways that are remembered forty years later? How did he become wise? These are the questions we must ask of ourselves, if we are to achieve the final imperative in Corporate Concinnity: Cultivating Wisdom.

In his book *The Greatest Generation*, Tom Brokaw argues that Mayor Harold's generation, remarkably characterized by "personal responsibility, duty, honor . . . faith . . . and humility," was a product of their circumstances: two world wars and the Great Depression. Are these important components of acquiring wisdom? Today's leaders have not lived those experiences. Is that why there seem to be more and more books on wisdom, while seemingly fewer truly wise people? Can it truly be that the Greatest Generation had a monopoly on wisdom? Will wisdom disappear as the memories of those who learned it slowly fade? Or is wisdom always there, available for those who seek it?

Finding Wisdom

I had dinner with an amazing man recently. He and his wife have been married for at least forty years and have three kids who seem to be doing really great things with their lives, and doing so independently. In this day and age, that seems to be a notable accomplishment, what with half of marriages ending in divorce and many of the younger generation "failing to launch." It is possible that I was so interested in listening to this man talk about his children because I have three twenty-somethings of my own who are in the early stages of preparing to do great things with their lives. But I think I was more intrigued by the *way* he spoke about how his children had come to be where they were, because as he spoke it was obvious that the interactions between this man and his children clearly impacted their success.

His was an inspiring story and a particular lesson for those of us who seek to lead and govern well.

Over the dinner table I felt as though I had a window into the conversations between those young people and their father. The communications were perceptive, insightful, understanding, and simultaneously demanding and grace-giving. Today's workplaces, the boardroom included, are demanding, if not excessively so. Far from being grace-giving, they can be relentless environments where no one is cutting slack for anyone else. What's missing in those settings and relationships is perception and insight combined with understanding and grace, and a shared accountability for the work of the whole. In a word, they are missing wisdom.

Who do you know who has wisdom? My father was wise. I think about him all the time, about his words to me, and yet he has been dead for years. Whose words do you think of when you try to recall wisdom? Whose words ring in your memory? For me there are not that many people: my father, a former executive coach, a handful of board colleagues, a few friends—that's all.

A common characteristic among the wise people I've known is that they were not perfect people. I knew them well enough to know that. But they were wise. And they offered me advice: wise counsel. They knew me and knew how to advise me. They helped me be a better me, a better person. But they also helped me be a better businessperson, a better executive. Interestingly, none of them walked a professional path exactly like my own. But each had walked thoughtfully down relevant experiences.

What if you thought about your boardroom from this

perspective: as a collection of wise people, committed to each other's best performance and growth? You are required to work together over an extended period of time on some pretty complex and potentially dramatic problems. Together, you will make decisions that impact the lives of your colleagues, employees, and clients or customers. What if you committed to mutual wisdom in your work? What would that mean? How would it look?

The board director committed to governing well will find the nine components of the concinnity framework for governance discussed thus far to be invaluable practices that will lead to greater effectiveness in governing. They will produce greater goodwill and fun in leading and governing and, in the process, drive greater performance. But they are practices that board members and their colleagues must do. They are ways of *doing*. By contrast, the tenth imperative in the framework is a way of *being*—the way of being wise. If the first nine imperatives are powerful tools in the kit of the board member, Imperative 10 is the duct tape, the one you can't live without, the one that holds it all together. Cultivating wisdom is essential for good governance. Unfortunately, it is something we don't think enough about.

> Wisdom is the duct tape in the toolkit of the corporate board; it is adhesion that holds the other nine imperatives together and makes them work.

Wisdom: Cognition, Reflection, and Compassion

Neuropsychologist Vivian Clayton, who has studied wisdom extensively, considers its essential elements to be cognition, reflection, and compassion. Let's look at each individually.

Cognitive functioning is something everyone does, right? After all, it is processing of information. It is about how much information we have, where to go if we need more, and how we assimilate, analyze, and put that information together in a coherent way. How fast do we do it? Faster is better, right? Wrong. Studies show that wisdom is more about *how* than *how fast*. Rather than being about speed, it is about the ability to connect dots: the ability to take data or raw or disparate information and convert it to decision-support information.

Three Components of Wisdom

- Cognition
- Reflection
- Compassion

Older people process more slowly. You will hear them, and likely their younger colleagues, complain about that. The reality is that older people have more information in their heads to process; they've been collecting it for decades! So, processing speed being equal, of course it would take them more time. In addition, however, the data in older brains is more nuanced, especially in the way it gets sorted and stored up, and as a result, the data in the mature brain is better suited to pattern recognition. Such minds and what they are able to process and produce make wisdom possible.

Reflection is the second component of wisdom. In Imperative 8 on coaching, we discussed the ability of a professional mentor to provide powerful, critical reflection.

Reflection and mature cognition are not things you can do quickly, because the first thing you must do is to stop. Then you have to step outside yourself and look at the situation from multiple perspectives.

"Multiple" is a key word here. It is critical to step outside of your own perspective. In order to do that effectively, you must have a different relationship with your own views and thoughts: one that is outside of your own emotional reactions, one that allows for assessing the situation with calm as opposed to hypersensitivity. You need to see the situation as one more puzzle to be solved, as opposed to a crisis over which to panic. Board members, and often their CEOs, must be the center of calm in storms, the ones with the steady hand on the rudder as change and crises are navigated.

Finally, wisdom involves compassion. This is also not so much something board members should do, as much as something they should *be*—more of a mindset or a way of being in their role as a director. One decides to be compassionate; it doesn't just happen, at least not for most of us. I talked about the role of reflection in moderating the emotion that can creep into how one sees a situation, especially a crisis. Compassion is really about injecting a certain kind of emotion—positive emotion as it pertains to other people. When one feels compassion for another person, it is hard to see that person as the embodiment of unsound thinking, or worse, malevolence, which goes a long way toward ensuring that situations are not seen as battlegrounds, but rather as opportunities to work together. I wrote earlier about generous listening and comparing and contrasting as tools to see the value in someone else or other ideas, a way to avoid being overly critical. Likewise these techniques can generate compassion. Compassion is a fundamental approach in the toolkit of the wise, one that is especially helpful during times of departure.

> Compassion is a fundamental approach in the toolkit of the wise, one that is especially helpful during times of departure.

Cultivating Wisdom

There was a study years ago about the personality types of company leadership at different levels of management. According to the study, those in middle management were by and large considered to be Type A people. Interestingly, those in executive management tested as Type B people. It was quite a paradox. Was it a classic story of the tortoise and the hare? Did the Type B folks outpace the Type As in the long run? Or did the Type A people find their Type B selves en route to the top? I think the latter is more likely. Type B folks are more focused on relationships and being than on accomplishments and doing. These Type B folks cultivated the wisdom that was in them.

I spoke recently with a board member who was telling me about a new CEO they hired. The CEO called this board member—a lot. Actually, make that "all the time." From the board member's perspective, the CEO was unable to make a decision. From my perspective, it was clear the CEO was looking for wisdom—from his board. This situation was a case study on many levels, but it was particularly relevant to how one seeks and cultivates wisdom in the boardroom and the C-suite. Wisdom requires the following:

1. Making good decisions;
2. Managing yourself;
3. Mature acceptance of consequences.

Part of wisdom is, of course, making good decisions. But a big part of wisdom is the process by which a person arrives at her decisions. How does one aggregate the facts? (Perhaps not *all* of the facts, but all of the necessary facts.) How does one know when he or she needs to keep gathering, and when he or she has gathered enough? What is indecision but a loop of conversation—unproductive what-ifs that don't resolve the situation but rather increase fear without increasing clarity—playing over and over again in our heads?

In the situation above, the director felt the CEO was unable to make good decisions. On the other hand, I expect the CEO felt the director was unwilling to share wisdom. I am sure the truth was somewhere in between. Greater harmony and shared decision making could have occurred had there been more conversation about each of their thoughts about how their communications were going.

A large part of wisdom is knowing how to manage yourself. In this case, the director would argue the CEO did not manage himself well. Sometimes it is helpful just to ask the question about self-management. We ask it about others all the time. Self-management includes your decision-making process, but it goes beyond that. It includes managing your own feelings, emotions, and confidence as you go about making inquiries, devising solutions, arriving at decisions, and leading. It also involves managing yourself, your emotions, once the decision is made.

Wise people have a totally different relationship with the consequences, both of their behaviors and of things outside their control. They realize that not only are there plenty of things outside of their control, but also that their work is done within a community and their views are just one component of the picture, the action, or the solution. They see the reality of limits when trying to control consequences. Once you accept those limits, it is easier to accept consequences, even when they are not exactly as you would wish. Wise leaders accept their successes and their failures, which also helps in the management of emotions. It is like the Serenity Prayer:

> God, grant me the serenity to accept the things I cannot change,
>
> The courage to change the things I can,
>
> And the wisdom to know the difference.[34]

So how can we cultivate wisdom? Seek out wise people. Listen to them. Consider your own decision making—actions, emotions, relationships—and their consequences. All of these things will help. Seeking out a professional mentor or executive mentor, wisely chosen, can also be an invaluable way to nurture wisdom.

But the mature leaders who are truly already wise understand that cultivating wisdom is an ongoing practice. They understand the necessity of learning as a lifelong activity. It's not that they know what we don't know. It's that they *know they don't know* many things. And they are ever eager to close the gaps in their learning. They don't fear asking questions. They seek out wise people to help them find the answers.

....

34 The "Serenity Prayer" is the common name for a prayer authored by the American theologian Reinhold Niebuhr (1892–1971). It has been adopted by Alcoholics Anonymous and other twelve-step programs.

Communicating Wisely in the Boardroom

My father used to say to my high-voiced little niece with some regularity, "Modulate, Kate." Born and raised in, and a resident of the South for all of his ninety-two years, my father was a stickler for the proper use of the human voice. He was convinced that if any of his children presented themselves outside of the South with full Southern drawls, we would promptly be dismissed as ignorant. So when I attended my first "mixer" in Boston as a college freshman, I was mortified when, after speaking approximately ten words to an attractive young man, he asked, "What part of the South are you from?" I made pretty quick work of losing the accent. After years of living in Connecticut, my late husband would tell me that I only slipped on three occasions: 1) when I was really tired, 2) when I had had a long visit with relatives (even on the phone!), or 3) when I had had a wee bit too much wine.

My father's words, ever in my brain, are well heeded by the wise, both about modulation in the use of the human voice and the use of the spoken word. They are particularly well heeded when trying to work constructively with board members. People miscommunicate in the boardroom all the time. They don't hear each other because they don't listen generously, but also because directors often communicate poorly. I have heard many directors complain that their ideas were not heeded, or worse, were claimed by someone else in the boardroom. Sometimes that may be intentional, and when that is the case the whole board must deal with it. But often it is because of untimely or poor conveyance of concerns and ideas.

> Modulation is an inflection of the tone or pitch of the voice, and regulating according to measure or proportion.

Speaking truth to power, as my colleagues define what we do, does not work without the right delivery. And that delivery depends on modulation.

The companion piece to modulating with success is listening. By listening, the process of defining problems becomes a joint exercise, a team effort. Discovery becomes mutual, not handed down from on high or outside. Once discovered together, there is less resistance to acknowledgment of problems, and together solutions can be crafted. This approach enables participants to modulate their voices when making contributions to defining problems and making suggestions based on ideas contributed by everyone.

When this happens, truth is discovered together. Solutions become shared creations. Voices avoid the shrill expression of judgment, because they naturally modulate down when all are working toward discovery. They modulate up only when discovery hits a dead end. And voices avoid the uneducated tenor of someone who doesn't know what wise people know. Modulating allows for avoiding the double sins of communicating too lightly and too harshly. And in the process—the process of listening and discovering together, of inviting participation—people get buy-in. This concurrence comes in a more constructive fashion than conversations started with such statements as, "I have some issues I need to raise with you, okay?" That may lead to verbal buy-in, but more often it sets up emotional closedown.

Natural and Nurtured Wisdom

When you think about it, the entire framework for concinnity in governing at the corporate level is all about wisdom: about having the cognition to connect the dots in a different way, to see governing as an opportunity to create a harmonious entity. It's about slowing down to see things differently, and to reflect upon them. And perhaps above all, it is about the willingness to be compassionate, especially when those around you are not. Were it possible to measure, wisdom would be at the top of my board expertise matrix. Were it possible to observe in action in advance of working together, I would add it to my "other touchy-feely skills" list of qualities for which to screen new board members. Neither measurement nor observation in advance is usually possible, but no doubt we recognize this quality in those we know well, and in those we sometimes meet, who seem to demonstrate wisdom. Perhaps it is gravitas. Is it a natural-born quality? I do not know. I do know that it can be cultivated.

A man living is yielding and receptive.
Dying, he is rigid and inflexible.
All things, the grass and trees:
Living, they are yielding and fragile;
Dying, they are dry and withered.
Thus those who are firm and inflexible
Are in harmony with dying.
Those who are yielding and receptive
Are in harmony with living.
Therefore an inflexible strategy will not triumph;
An inflexible tree will be attacked.
The position of the highly inflexible will descend;
The position of the yielding and receptive will ascend.

The *Tao Te Ching* by Lao Tzu, Chapter 76

Translated by R. L. Wing, 1986

Conclusion

IN LATE 1984 the staffs of both the National League of Women Voters and the National Football League were busy going about their respective businesses. Unbeknownst to them, their worlds were about to collide.

The NLWV was hard at work getting agreement between the campaign staffs of Walter Mondale and Ronald Reagan on the particulars of the fall presidential debates, something which, I understand, is about as easy as negotiating a major trade agreement. At long last the dates were settled and the staff went about the process of notifying the media.

Almost immediately the president of the League of Women Voters received a phone call from a senior executive with ABC television. As it turns out, ABC had the rights to broadcast the Sunday night NFL games that year, and the campaigns and the NLWV had picked a time for one of the debates that conflicted with an already scheduled NFL game.

The ABC executive was in a real pickle, and he let that be known in no uncertain terms. ABC was contractually obligated to the NFL to broadcast the game; violating that contract would have cost the network millions of dollars. But broadcasting in a time slot conflicting with the presidential debates amounted to public relations suicide. He was hoping to convince the League of Women Voters to change dates. The reality was that the NLWV president was between her own rock and hard place: Bringing the Mondale and Reagan campaigns back to the negotiating table would be no easier than renegotiating an NFL broadcasting contract.

So the president of the League of Women Voters had a better idea, much to the shock of ABC. Why not just call the NFL commissioner and talk it over? Undoubtedly a good percentage of the NFL audience wanted to watch the debates and, no doubt, there were plenty of voters who would be torn between the debates and the game, which is to say these two leaders had a number of stakeholders in common. They needed a skillful, harmonious, and elegant way to piece together the various parts of this shared dilemma. They needed concinnity.

And they got it. With the help of the commissioner, the debates were moved up half an hour and the game was moved back. Everyone gave a little, and everybody won.

This story was retold at the retirement dinner of a board colleague of mine. Although we had served with her for years, few of us knew of her service as president of the National League of Women Voters—or of the story above. It is just one of many testaments to her wisdom and leadership. It is also a tale of concinnity in leading and governing. Each of the leaders in this story let go of command and control and worked to put together a solution that would bring their overlapping stakeholders into harmony.

From this story alone it is clear they practiced at least six of the imperatives for Corporate Concinnity in governing.

They:

1. Were clear on their respective roles,

2. Assembled the right people around the table to work constructively toward a solution,

3. Understood where they were, where they needed to go, and how to get there,

4. Tended to the interests of diverse stakeholders,

5. Dealt constructively with the change that landed in their laps, and

6. Showed real wisdom.

To use a baseball analogy, this team hit six out of the ten Corporate Concinnity imperatives. Rather than seeing that as just 60 percent, I suggest we see it as an unbelievable batting average—.600—in the game of Corporate Concinnity. It is a game that is played over a career—a journey—and one that these players obviously mastered. Achieving Corporate Concinnity is something leaders must work at every day, just like baseball players.

If you have been around business a while, you no doubt are familiar with failure. If you have been around a long while, I'd guess you have seen, if not experienced, a few of the failures of conventional thinking about governance. In all likelihood, you have been up close and personal with the ten common mistakes the concinnity framework is designed to avoid. The framework I describe comes from years of watching the best do it right and, in the process, far outperform their peers. I have also seen many do it wrong, and struggle to succeed. The Ten Imperatives are in reality the antidote for the most common things boards and CEOs do wrong as they seek to govern together.

Governing with concinnity is not an exercise in altruism. While I like to think of myself as kind, I am no altruist; I am all about performance. Living in and working with scores of companies and leaders over the years helped me develop this framework for a better way of governing the corporation. And as I said, nothing should be more important to you than how you build exceptional, sustainable leadership teams, effective governance platforms, and a strategy to make them work well together. When you do, you and your colleagues will be far more effective. Your company will outperform its competition, if not its previous metrics. And you all will have more fun.

The forward-thinking board member, C-suite executive, family business owner, and investor are committed to excellence and continuous improvement in governance. They will be very well served by embracing the Corporate Concinnity framework. High-performing companies of the future will be characterized by it, and how we govern together as leaders will become as important as the changes already occurring in the *who* and *what* of corporate governance—if not more so. The accelerating pace of change and disruption, the emergence of more and more complex risks, and the need to find opportunities in the midst of all this demand no less. In the process of driving results, the Corporate Concinnity framework's nine practical, tangible things boards can do, combined with the tenth imperative—a way of being, of *wisdom*—can radically change the effectiveness of the board's work and can drive constructive harmony in the boardroom and with the CEO and her team. The outcome will be not only vastly improved corporate performance, but also relationships that are far more enjoyable.

Enjoy!

Acknowledgments

GOOD LEADERSHIP AND good governance are journeys that committed people make together. The wisdom I have shared in this book has been gathered over the years as I have worked with incredible colleagues and clients from around the globe. There would be no framework for governing with Corporate Concinnity without the experiences I have gained partnering with the wise, the flawed, the patient, the frustrated, the searching, and the creative. It goes without saying that they are too numerous to name, but they own the lessons herein as much as I do. If you've ever worked with me you probably appear somewhere in this book and deserve some of the credit. Many have blessed me with trust, respect, patience, and generosity as we have journeyed together to improve complex organizations in ways that honor differences and harness diversity to solve problems creatively, elegantly, and harmoniously weaving together all the pieces of the puzzle. This work has been a gift.

It has been almost thirty years since I held my first board chair position. In that role I was privileged to work with CEO Jane Norgren, who modeled Corporate Concinnity before I realized it was a thing that needed a name. Thank you, Jane, for your wisdom, partnership, and for launching my passion for finding a better way to solve hard problems in complex organizations.

To the numerous forward-thinking board members, CEOs, and C-suite members who have allowed me to help them see what they could not see on their own, and who had faith in our process to produce positive outcomes and value, I will be forever grateful.

This book would still be a blog without the encouragement of the incredible team at Greenleaf Book Group, from founder Clint Greenleaf who encouraged me to work with his team, to Carolyn "you are in my head" Roark, whose editorial advice came with wining, dining, and chauffeur services, to Scott James and the team that brought smart marketing to the table on day one. Greenleaf is an author's one-stop-shopping dream.

I want to thank Tom and Cathy Rogerson for the loan of the Author's Lair and its two adorable muses, Chief and Wrigley; Kris Kaligian for texting me with timely advice on breaking and entering; Elta Falls Mariani for making lunches; Angeline Falls Mariani for hosting the editing retreat; and Noel Price, whose energy and passion to change the world inspires me daily to try to do the same from the halls of corporate America.

Thanks also go to writing-discipline and covenant-partner Dr. Diana Sharp for helping me keep the faith and stay on track.

I am grateful for Michael Lalor's generous and thoughtful work as a beta reader and for numerous other former Tatum partners who shared war stories from their C-suite and board-room adventures.

I want to thank Karen Steadman, executive coach extraordinaire, for making me a better leader and for her ongoing encouragement.

I am thankful to have had three personal boards of directors over the years that have been my most up-close and personal advisors—two in New England and one in Nashville. Mothers Who Work Outside the Home: You know who you are and I am here because of you. Jugglers: You rock. Wellesley sisters: Thank you for practicing what Henry Fowle and Pauline Durant preached, "Non ministrari, sed ministrare." I am glad I have been able to provide ongoing challenges for you to help solve. Just remember, I know you as well as you know me.

I want to thank Debbie Ahl for her time and insight as a beta reader, for believing that Corporate Concinnity is a real thing—a true business need—and for joining me in co-creating the pivot in my work that has produced The Concinnity Company. Thank you Corbette Doyle for the connection and for sharing your popcorn machine of ideas.

Thank you Michelle Privee for bailing me out of Internet and document hell with unfailing good cheer and for your skillful and creative way of presenting things. Thank you Meredith Lawrence and Kendal Beahm for keeping me social.

And most of all I want to thank Neil for, well, everything.

About the Author

LEADERSHIP AND GOVERNANCE expert Nancy Falls helps drive companies' success by transforming the way boards and leadership teams work together. She has spent over 30 years in and around the C-suite and the boardroom, having held executive roles in both public and private companies, from early stage to multi-billion dollar global enterprises, served on numerous boards, including as Board Chair, advised some of the largest healthcare and industrial companies in America and coached dozens of C-level executives. A magna cum laude graduate in economics and sociology from Wellesley College, Falls is a Governance Fellow of the National Association of Corporate Directors. She and her family live in Nashville, where she is CEO of The Concinnity Company.

Find out more about building powerful
leadership-govenance teams at
www.theconcinnitycompany.com